Letters to Momo

Letters
to Momo

A Remarkable Story
About the Power
to Overcome

Alejandro Souza

NEW YORK

Letters to Momo
A Remarkable Story About the Power to Overcome

Published in New York, New York, by Morgan James Publishing. Morgan James and The Entrepreneurial Publisher are trademarks of Morgan James, LLC. www.MorganJamesPublishing.com

The Morgan James Speakers Group can bring authors to your live event. For more information or to book an event visit The Morgan James Speakers Group at www.TheMorganJamesSpeakersGroup.com.

"Your Seed Pouch," "The Violin," and "You're It," copyright 1999 by Daniel Ladinsky, from *The Gift: Poems by Hafiz* (Penguin, 1999), and reprinted by permission of Daniel Ladinsky.

FREE eBook edition for your existing eReader with purchase

PRINT NAME ABOVE

For more information, instructions, restrictions, and to register your copy, go to www.bitlit.ca/readers/register or use your QR Reader to scan the barcode:

ISBN 978-1-61448-769-2 paperback
ISBN 978-1-61448-770-8 eBook
ISBN 978-1-61448-771-5 audio
Library of Congress Control Number: 2013945575

Cover Design by:
Chris Treccani
www.3dogdesign.net

Interior Design by:
Bonnie Bushman
bonnie@caboodlegraphics.com

In an effort to support local communities, raise awareness and funds, Morgan James Publishing donates a percentage of all book sales for the life of each book to Habitat for Humanity Peninsula and Greater Williamsburg.

Get involved today, visit
www.MorganJamesBuilds.com

Habitat for Humanity®
Peninsula and Greater Williamsburg
Building Partner

To my mother
Each word written is but a mere echo
of your towering courage, love and example

Contents

He who has a why to live
can endure any how
Friedrich Nietzsche

Acknowledgments

This book would have never been published without the consent and blessing of my dearest cousin Momo. He is a statue of courage that epitomizes the power of vulnerability. I am forever grateful and in awe of his inspiring selflessness—a true warrior poet. We are all in his debt for choosing to share his story and extend a loving hand for all who choose to walk alongside us.

In order to publish this book, I launched a crowd-sourcing campaign on Kickstarter. I owe a very special debt of gratitude to the amazing 247 backers who pledged their financial and emotional support for the campaign. Thanks to their belief and conviction, I was able to edit and proofread the final manuscript, purchase 2,500 books for my own distribution, translate the book into Spanish, and eventually donate 200 books to prisons, rehabilitation centers, homeless shelters, and other support centers all over the world. They are the very ink that brought this book to life. This is just the beginning. Our dream is bigger and bolder. With their incredible help, we've already unleashed a movement to walk together.

Here are the precious 247 backers, in the order in which they pledged their support:

1. Renata Souza Luque
2. Mariana Souza
3. Alejandro Adler Braun
4. Adriana Peon
5. Jessica Johnston
6. Daniel Vogel
7. Maria del Carmen Perez
8. Laura Budzyna
9. Mariana Costa
10. Gerald McElroy
11. Marisol Alarcon
12. Miguel Rivera
13. Luis Yañez
14. Ignacio Urrutia
15. Nitesh Mayani
16. Sarah Snidal
17. Deborah Spindelman
18. Yazmin Delgado
19. Karla Olivares Souza
20. Jeronimo Olivares
21. AJ Leon
22. Paloma Ruiz González
23. Jimena Souza
24. Mariana Courtney
25. Luis Pedro Revilla
26. Herman Marin
27. Wing Huo
28. Estefania Souza Luque
29. Max Adler
30. Christina Feng
31. Paul Runge
32. Analuz Vizarretea
33. Stefanie Wedy
34. Mike Abadi
35. Sebastien Carreau
36. Monica Olivares
37. Angela Jacques
38. Tessy Michan
39. Sandra Creixell
40. Jose Acero
41. Diana Fridman
42. Caoilfhionn de Bhaldraithe
43. Juan Ossa
44. Consuelo Cruz
45. Len Schlesinger
46. Stephanie Foote
47. Yotam Dankner
48. Armida Yuriar
49. Martin Schoenhals
50. Carolina Ocampo-Maya
51. Mona Jaber
52. Brendan Foote
53. Lauren Salay
54. Lourdes Pintado
55. Graciela Blanchet
56. Shahbano Tirmizi

57. Marino Ossa-Eslait
58. Patrick Harmon
59. Canaria Gaffar
60. Pedro Toro
61. Jaime Buc
62. Christopher Planicka
63. Alejandra Ucros
64. Emma Violet Makinson
65. Anna Richardson
66. Mariana Iturriaga
67. Pablo Friedman de Souza
68. Mario Adler
69. Carlos Flores
70. Lola Iturbe
71. Melissa Martinez
72. Christian Barrett
73. Alejandra Lopez
74. Rodrigo Paz y Rocha
75. Mariana Becerra
76. Moy Schwartzman
77. Cristina Acevedo
78. Nancy Gaggino
79. Josue Garza
80. Tanya Wattnem
81. Karon Olvera Garza
82. Ana Bernal Stuart
83. Gabriela Rocha
84. Carlos Fuentevilla
85. Tania Grinberg
86. Alonso Alvarez
87. Leena Khan

88. Cecilia Herrerías Brunel
89. Martin Urrutia
90. Ashley King
91. Alejandro J. Maiz M
92. Norma Torregrosa
93. Vera Martínez
94. Gabriel Margolis
95. Venetia Aranha
96. José Calderón
97. Lorena Gonzalez
98. Jaivardhan Singh
99. Ben Salinas
100. Lukas Montoya Burgos
101. Kathleen Sims
102. Katrina Fincher
103. Eve Konstantine
104. Nadine Elias
105. Lakshmi Balachandran
106. Moy Romano
107. Jeronimo Lebrija
108. Gabriela Harmon
109. Ariel Lebowitz
110. Lorenzo Lagos
111. Megann Mielke
112. Ernesto Lopez Ortega
113. Alexandra Howland
114. Rodrigo Ferreira
115. Brenda Ciuk
116. Nora Zenczak
117. Nicolás Argüello
118. Lucía Gamboa

119. Christine Vinette
120. Gaby Lopez Benavides
121. Manuel Wiechers Banuet
122. Demetrio Ramírez Gomez
123. Danielle Sobol
124. Danielle Romano
125. Andrea Marcos
126. Víctor Angel
127. Joaquin Hirschfeld Mereles
128. Matt Boynton
129. Sara Miracco
130. Leonor Cusi
131. Priscila Garcia Gutierrez
132. Marcia Stein
133. Claudia Gutierrez
134. Oscar Quintero
135. Bruno Meli
136. Manasi Hukku
137. Catalina Kulczar-Marin
138. Tatiana Gonzalez Fernandez
139. Yosune Rodriguez
140. Daniela Yañez
141. Juan M. Aguero
142. Ramses Franco
143. Columba Yañez
144. Bryan Miller
145. Baerbel Huepen
146. Alexandra Violante
147. Gerri Randlett
148. Joyce Wong
149. Anu Halonen
150. Alexa Webster
151. Flavia Hentsch
152. Alejandro Ehrenberg
153. Marcela Gutierrez
154. Fernando Madrazo
155. Raul Marquez Pardinas
156. Alejandro Chanona
157. Daniel Barrera
158. Lian Zhang
159. Sarah Sukumaran
160. Soha Ehsani
161. Allie Rathert
162. Melissa Veytia
163. Ana Celinda Sendel
164. Kathryn Waller
165. Andrea Wild
166. Carlyn Cowen
167. Max Owen
168. Heberto Alvarado Cuesta
169. Rafael Merchan
170. Julio Souza
171. Miriam Antoun
172. Kanan Mehra
173. Edu Herrera
174. Maria Fernanda Ballesteros
175. Will Cross
176. María Soledad Valencia
177. Eyal Agai
178. Dalinda Perez Alvarez
179. Amy K. Salay
180. Laura Lebrija Villarreal

181. Carolina Corrales
182. Katherine Rockwell
183. Mara Castillo
184. Elizabeth Dearborn Davis
185. David L. Hancock
186. Kathylee Culver Forrester
187. Paul Donner
188. Mariana Urdaibay
189. Mireya Lopez
190. Rodulfo Prieto
191. Minty Castilla
192. Caitlin Rackish
193. Amber Neko
194. Ignacio Armillas
195. Alejandra Garcia Peña Carvallo
196. Arturo Ortega Lomelin
197. Julian Gabriel Souza
198. Quinn Marshall
199. Alfredo De La Hoz
200. Alina Alcantara
201. Sandra Avila-Gamio
202. Alexander Ehrenberg S
203. Nelly Gomez
204. Melissa Watson
205. Ellen Bello
206. Loren Bernal
207. Susana Gabriela Souza
208. Jonathan Caspi Miller
209. Fabio Montenegro
210. Iñigo Villamil
211. Giovanni Cocom Tah
212. Andrew Abitbol
213. Lydia B. White
214. Mariel Calderón
215. Rodrigo García Valles
216. Paco Villalpando Lorda
217. Guillermo Cañedo Malburg
218. Linet Suarez
219. Alejandro Porteny
220. Juan Miguel Marin
221. Jill Anderson and Nin Solis
222. Mariel Wiechers
223. Till Coster and John Pike
224. Alexia Nunez
225. Debbie Aizenman
226. Jamie Phua
227. Mathias Stroers
228. Alejandro Santoyo
229. Itziar Diez-Canedo
230. Diego Flores
231. Angelica Creixell
232. Cameron McKenzie
233. Patricio Suarez
234. Elsa Gomez de Gil
235. Yianni Douros
236. María Díaz Anaya
237. Rosamaría Alanís
238. Olga Nuñez
239. Costa Cumaná
240. Eduardo Landa
241. Mauricio Oltra

I could not have written a single word of this book had I not been shaped by my mother for twenty-four years before I wrote the first letter. I owe the greatest parts of who I am to her inspirational love, mentoring, fortitude, and wisdom. Honestly, it is impossible for me to distinguish her words from mine, as they all originate from the same masterpiece that is her life. I cannot imagine a greater gift than the opportunity to learn from her.

Alejandro Adler, my friend, brother, and fellow tripper, is a radiant emblem of walking together. Because our paths always run parallel, his support, strength, and trust stood by me and dignified each step of this and all processes. He read each letter immediately after I wrote it, living and celebrating the experience with unmatched human empathy. His friendship is the manifested certainty of all I could ever dream and dare to write about.

Luis Yañez, the Mexican embodiment of "Captain America," is a true superhero amongst us mortals. Effortlessly, he personifies far too many virtues that most spend a lifetime chasing in vain. He shot, edited, and perfected the campaign's video with a loud smile on his face.

Ignacio Urrutia is the big brother whom all families the world over would feel overwhelmingly blessed to have. A warmly vigilant and fervent seeker of truth, Ignacio's unyielding values contain, understand, and enable the intellectual and emotional development of so many. Reassuringly, he reminded me how to believe again when it all felt strangely out of grasp—making every step that much easier to take.

I am grateful to my publisher, David Hancock, and his team at Morgan James Publishing for their support and empowering service. I am grateful also to my editor, Amanda Rooker, and her team for their warm and careful editing of the manuscript. They managed to simultaneously maintain the letters' original cadence and voice while ensuring they became even more audible.

Finally, a special thanks to literary agent Michael Ebeling. Willingly and gracefully, Michael volunteered his help and time, introduced me to my publisher, encouraged me, and guided and advised me on how to best navigate the daunting world of publishing. Michael is a true angel in the industry.

Written FOR ONE

Published BY MANY

INSPIRING FOR ALL

Introduction

The letters found in this book refer to a particular experience in my life. Then again, they address much more than that single experience. They address my entire life.

I was born into a loving family and raised lovingly by devoted parents. Of course, I wasn't the perfect child. Like most children, one day I found myself punished in my room for having misbehaved. I remember lying on my bed and thinking to myself, "Consider this training, in case one day when you are older and you are off soldiering in some distant battle, you are taken captive. This is what prison must feel like." I should probably mention that I was rather melodramatic at the time. Nevertheless, that thought crossed my mind, and I pondered it.

During my second year at university, I was sentenced to nine months in prison, of which I served five. Without a doubt, this was the most unexpected and challenging experience I had ever faced, not only because of the obvious reason that prison isn't something to dream about while lying in bed as a child, but because during this time I was coming out of a deep depression that had lasted over a year. So here I am now, sitting at home, typing away on my laptop in an attempt to introduce you to what I consider to be one of the reasons why my time spent in prison, both physically at HMP Liverpool and mentally during my depression, has been one of the most empowering experiences in my life: the contents of my cousin's letters.

First I would like to take this opportunity to express my reasons for wanting to publish these letters. Although these letters are addressed to me, the message is addressed to everyone. Imprisonment takes many shapes. I experienced one form of it during my paralyzing depression, and another within a prison cell in a foreign country. Throughout my life, I have met people who are or have once been challenged, worn down, and chained by mental and spiritual prisons. Others have had to live a life limited and crippled by a physical handicap, which has had deep consequences upon their outlook on life. This is what is of great importance in the end: our outlook on it all. And it is exactly this outlook that these letters explore.

It would be unfair for me to call these letters a source of encouragement, because they are far more than that. They are a stream of consciousness sent out as a reminder. They are what you have always known, yet perhaps never understood: that you are divine by nature and nothing you can do can change that. You can only forget it and thus disconnect yourself from the source within and without you. These letters are a rekindling.

In the face of any adversity, it is our interpretation and our reaction that forges the outcome of the battle between self and circumstance. These letters are a call to action, a beckoning to the realization that we are authors and our lives are our story. Each thought that we pinch out of the canvas of our mind makes up the ink that writes the novel. We should then choose wisely and bravely. These letters are an invitation to a journey of both discovery and re-acquaintance, of liberation and celebration.

Today, I am grateful for the opportunity to share them with you, and I pray they become as significant to you as they were to me.

Now, let us walk together.

Momo

Preface

I wrote these letters because nobody should walk alone.

In September of 2010, I received an email informing me that my cousin Momo, as I called him, had been imprisoned. His situation was deeply challenging to say the least: twenty-three years old and about to graduate from university abroad, his world was suddenly confined to one of Her Majesty's largest prisons in Liverpool. His parents and sisters were all home in Mexico, an Atlantic Ocean away.

A truly compassionate, loving, and caring person only a year my junior, Momo has always been my closest friend in the family. Although we lived in different countries most of our lives, no physical distance ever kept us from connecting and feeling close. I soon learned that his sentence actually began approximately one month prior. To spare us from the pain, anguish, and uncertainty of arduous legal proceedings, Momo had requested his family not be told anything until the sentencing was final. Crushed by his imprisonment and the realization that he had already been facing this situation alone for a month or more, I made an unconditional commitment to live the experience as close to him as I possibly could.

My mind was made up: I resolved to write him one letter each day for as long as he was in jail.

My daily letters were my way of walking with Momo and infusing him with strength, resilience, and above all, love. I wrote the letters to help him not only survive the incarceration, but to transcend it by consciously seeking the value of the experience as a platform for liberation and growth.

Never brooding or negative, I wrote each letter with a positive and inspiring tone as an empowering reminder that he was not a victim of circumstance, and that if he chose to, he could author the change he desired in his life. In short, the letters were intended to rouse the personal power to overcome that we each are innately born with.

Although I was informed that he was indeed receiving the letters, I had no way of knowing the effect they had or if they were even welcome. Due to the inefficiency of the prison communication channels, I only heard back from him once, toward the final weeks of his sentence. Some days, this silence made the task of writing a single letter disheartening. Needless to say, I knew that any mundane obstacle I faced was inferior and potentially insignificant when compared to Momo's tribulations. Accordingly, my commitment to walk by his side remained stronger than any apparent challenge, and so I pushed on.

Still, on some days, life's unprecedented twists and turns left me unable to write a letter. These scattered and minimum interruptions occurred mostly on weekends or due to trips, urgent work demands, a brief stomach infection, and a few otherwise haphazard events. Fortunately, it was later brought to my attention that these intermittent pauses proved beneficial, as they granted Momo a space to digest, reflect, and apply some of the letters' core messages.

The first letter was by far the hardest to write. Every other key typed was interrupted by a steady, all-consuming, yet cathartic flow of tears. After a few minutes though, the process of writing even that first letter became enjoyable. From then on, each letter I wrote detonated a profound and liberating experience, which I was eager to relive every day. Rather than representing a wearisome burden despite its pure intention, the task of writing was intensely gratifying, because each letter was written straight from the heart in genuine stream-of-consciousness. As a result, I felt, lived, embodied, and channeled every word I wrote prior to it being manifested on the screen in front of me. Each uplifting thought I wrote lifted me up in tandem.

I wanted to make sure Momo received the most visceral version of my being in that particular moment. I thought that by rendering this distinctively sincere, approachable, and contemplative exhibition of my innermost emotional and rational firings, the vitality of each thought and feeling would somehow be magically transported from my computer to his cell—and be entirely relived by him upon reading.

My method of writing reminds me of an essential philosophical tenet of Chinese calligraphy I once researched in high school: the "One Breath" technique. Master Chinese calligraphers believed that by starting and finishing each piece in one continuous brushstroke without any hesitation, they would ensure the work had rhythmic vitality. To break the flow, if only for a second, meant to compromise the work's spiritual potency and kill its life force.

This notion is what drove me to write all the letters in just a few minutes. I never stopped to review punctuation or general structure and rarely reread a letter prior to sending it. Evidently, honoring each letter's unique life force became the fuel, guide, and reason for writing. In this sense, although the letters were never written with the intention of being published, or for anyone other than Momo, I somehow wrote these letters to parts of myself as well.

Thus intentionally, the letters share no implicit link regarding content, themes, or messages. The letters' contemplations span from personal experience to cognitive psychology, probe spiritual verses of Persian poets such as Hafez and Rumi, and explore principles of courage and liberation from Friedrich Nietzsche to Saint-Exupery's *The Little Prince*. At times, however, I would find myself referring to or redeveloping some ideas explored in previous letters. Nevertheless, most letters might appear to be just as random as my unique thought processes, sensations, and meditations from the day that gave them birth. What each letter does share is the same unyielding objective: to craft a positive voyage of introspection that reignites our innate divinity.

Many letters and a few months later, Momo was released from prison and flew back to Mexico City. Once home, he finally told me face-to-face how important the letters had been. He told me the letters became his lifeline, that they gave him love and strength to overcome his physical and psychological prisons, to find meaning in his experience, and to ultimately achieve personal growth and liberation.

Momo and I first discussed the idea of publishing the letters over lunch just a couple of weeks after his release. At the beginning, he was understandably hesitant. As Momo mentioned, the letters were so special to him that he had ascribed a sort of ownership over them. He rightly felt they were his, and the thought of sharing them with the world, for numerous reasons, made him uncomfortable.

The more we spoke about it, the more we realized that the power behind the letters could be useful to anyone at any time in their lives. Contrary to what he initially felt, Momo then told me it would be a blessing to share them with the world, because there is no ownership to such sincere insights. He then decided he wanted to publish the letters, realizing his experience is a microcosm of human liberation.

With this sentiment in our hearts, we agreed to publish the letters due to the power of their message and their story, but most importantly because we are certain they can inspire and empower others to confront and overcome barriers to their own liberation, regardless of situation or background.

This book is the collection of all the daily letters I wrote to my cousin Momo—exactly as he received them.

The letters remain intact in their original state, as pure as originally sent to Momo, and in the same order he read them. That's how they worked for him, and with hope, that's how they'll work for us all.

This book is less about the art of telling and more about the art of exploring. I offer this book as an invitation for you to choose to experience a journey of renewed choices. A choice to face yourself whimsically, to dig fearlessly, to own the change you envision, and to walk, wholeheartedly, with yourself and with others. Allow the additive virtue of each choice to catalyze your own personal story of resilience, transcendence, and freedom. Enjoy your story, and let it remind you of your heroic life force and rhythmic vitality.

Today, let these letters walk with you.

May 2013

New York

Part I
September 2010

*The ultimate value of life
depends upon awareness and
the power of contemplation
rather than upon mere survival*

Aristotle

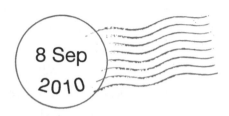

8 Sep
2010

My dearest brother Momo,

This is a very difficult email to write as tears stream down my face. This is
the absolute first and only time I will comment on the negative aspects of
this situation, for my emails are designed to hopefully shed some positive
light instead, a lot of love, and true and honest companionship, from my
heart to yours. I simply need you to know that I am feeling absolutely
everything for you, that my empathy for your situation is very profound
and real, and that I am very, deeply sorry that you have to go through
this, that this is a situation in your life that needs to be lived, and that you
find yourself where you are now. Rest assured that all will pass and that
your life will be blessed beyond belief as a result of this, through this, and
because of this. I know it can be very difficult to see and believe this right
now, but only time will remove all masks of doubt, hatred, suspicion,
anger, and guilt, leaving only understanding, peace of mind, virtue, and
above all else love. Above all love.

Momo, I want you to know that I have decided to live this experience
with you every step of the way, as your brother, walking next to your

every stride, rejoicing in your meditations, sharing your thoughts and feelings, and offering always a warm embrace, a loving smile, and all the support and fortitude you could possibly need. I am here for you, in every possible way, and I am making myself entirely available to you, within my inevitable limitations, so that together, we can walk through this. You are not alone, nor will ever be, and this is something you need to know in your heart, for this will be the solace that will put you to bed at night and the strength and wisdom needed to wake up and shine with the sun.

You might be in prison physically, but you can be anywhere you choose to be mentally, internally. Even in the darkest of times, in the hardest of moments, know in your heart that there is divine justice in everything. Everything is as it should be. This is not an attempt at false optimism; this is a reminder of our innate divinity, a call to action for the faith we seek to become, the force that drives us, and an honest acknowledgment of the truth within. Accept your situation with an open heart and an open mind, and be grateful for everything you have chosen and for everything that you have allowed yourself to experience.

Your soul needs this experience to grow, to learn, to become itself, and to then serve. Know this deep inside you because you are not a victim. No one in that prison is. A victim is powerless; a victim externalizes all self-worth and leaves it to the whims of those judging his situation, to the whims of the equally powerless left only to celebrate self-pity. No, yours is a world of endless opportunity, a rapturous gift of self-consciousness, a beautiful period of time left to internalize all, to reflect, to appreciate, to understand…and if you dare, to enjoy. For that is the ultimate battle, the warrior poet's last justice, the freedom, the opportunity to enjoy your current situation, to find that light, and to become it, because only you author the choice of perspective, only you can decide what world you will inhabit. This is a time to live and to let life once again take center stage while we remain loyally in awe, a faithful audience observing, participating, experiencing how it all simply is, how it all blends into each other, and how there is order, harmony, and perfect design, divine design, in absolutely everything.

This is your choosing, whether conscious or sub-conscious, and there is power in that! There is freedom in that for there is ownership, and where there is ownership, there is no guilt. Your situation carries absolutely no guilt: no self-guilt and no guilt externalized and placed on someone else. He who is thankful can rejoice in every situation, for the attention is in the brilliance of it—in what you see and realize, and in the gifts you give yourself, day in and day out, because you can. Because you choose to. Remember that what you invite in is what you acknowledge...choose wisely. Guilt is a rational construct, a product of cognition. It does not exist. Just as easily as it was constructed, so can it be destroyed. It all depends on you and on where your attention is, for where your attention lies, therein lies your energy, your being. Channel it wisely, channel to that which exists and not to a mental construct that is self-destructive. The same goes for pain and suffering. Pain exists; it is a metaphysical experience. If we bump our head on the wall, we will experience pain. We will pay attention to it as it happens, accept its presence, and then we will move on, and the pain will become nothing more than an occurrence, a memory.

You cannot, however, suffer from that bump on the head. Suffering is a choice; it is another mentally-constructed product of lingering in the past, on failing to see that the bump on the head came and went, that there is no more pain...suffering is mental pain fueled by angst, by self-deceit, and by lies. You cannot suffer unless you choose to. However, in that sentence lies a counter argument of equal power: you can only suffer if you feel you don't deserve happiness. Now we can easily rid ourselves of this claim, for it entails killing two non-existent rational products: guilt and suffering. And nothing is easier than killing things that don't exist, right? You simply stop paying attention to them, and they dissolve into

thin air. You will only feel you don't deserve happiness if you feel guilty…
if there is that mental construct obstructing your divine gift to freedom
and infinite happiness.

So you get rid of guilt, and automatically you re-open the real door,
the door to happiness, the door to truth, and the door to your life. So
how can you stop suffering? By feeling the PAIN and choosing to release
the mental construct of suffering. If we linger, we suffer; we freeze time
and space and cease to experience and to experiment with reality, as life is
happening in this moment. Choose to inhabit yourself wholly, in THIS
MOMENT ONLY, and leave everything else to the divine unknown,
with faith that we are being carried and guided accordingly.

I read something beautiful the other day: "we are the furthest away
from reality when we honestly believe there is a legitimate reason for us to
suffer". The furthest away from reality…well let's get the closest to reality
as possible! And to do that, we simply need to honestly believe there is
a legitimate reason to never suffer! A realization, an internal truth that
reminds us that we are not here to suffer! It's as easy as realizing that we
are innately divine! We are God's creatures! Do you think he wants us to
suffer? Impossible. That's all on us, that's our choice, and our disregard
for his ultimate beauty.

Momo, you are a beautiful human being, and I see nothing but
love, kindness, and absolute integrity in your soul. I love you deeply and
honestly, and I can see only the pure goodness and truth of your life! I
celebrate you, and I know who you are!

You must always remind yourself of this, always hold yourself
accountable for your own worth, because for us to see it you must see it
first and you must see it always! There is brilliance and strength in your
heart; I know this and that is why I am not worried for you. I know
you as a warrior, as a sacred warrior. This is simply another chapter in a
brilliant life; do not forget this. See it within the context of your entire
life, open up the lens, and expand the perspective; do not see it for its

limited definition and context only. And remember that nothing defines who you are. Nothing. The only things that can define you are your thoughts, your emotions, and your convictions. You are you forever, and I love you.

We are bound by love and by mutual understanding, so let's ignite this gift that we share, so that we can walk through this together. You are not alone, nor will you ever be. I will remind you constantly of this, so that you might receive all the love that I have received from you, always and unconditionally, because that is who you are, a channel of truth and brilliance, a true warrior.

Be a warrior, my brother. Flip this entire thing on its head by doing simply one thing: be grateful. That sheds light onto everything, and you will remain in peace. Be grateful. To be grateful, one must acknowledge the worth in things and magnify their power to your advantage. Lay your thoughts on that which is, in reality, in the space where suffering and guilt have no place, no reason to be, and absolutely no presence. Grant yourself the freedom to understand that this is exactly as it needs to be, for you have chosen to LIVE this experience, because only this could grant you the wisdom you needed to continue becoming.

Remember that life only throws us situations when we are ready for them; therefore you have everything already in your power to live through this situation, and moreover you have everything already in your power to turn this situation into a golden opportunity for whatever it is you might desire internally! There is nothing you need to do; you only have to allow its brilliance to manifest itself. Simply conduct yourself as a worthy channel by harnessing love, truth, and appreciation, and filtering away doubt, suffering, and guilt. I leave you for now with a huge smile, my brother, for love prevails over everything, and because, as a warrior, your freedom, your strength, and your honor are forever yours, and will forever be brilliant and present.

I love you with all my heart, and today, let me walk with you.

My dearest brother Momo,

First of all, I want to send you an enormous smile, covering my entire face. Please picture it now. Now take that smile and put it on your face, for yours is mine and mine is yours! Life is truly simple when we choose to focus on the essential…just like in *The Little Prince*, when Saint-Exupéry says, "Only with the heart does one see rightly; what's essential is invisible to the eye." The essence is love, and it's love shared and channeled that makes us more than human, makes us divine, and thus divinely human! The Little Prince was talking to his favorite rose upon saying those words…a rose who needed the heart as a correspondent, not the eye. You have a correspondent here, my brother, from my heart to yours. Today is a beautiful day and it's yours, entirely! Just like a fantastic mystery, the clues for divine beauty are scattered everywhere; all are within love, but you need the heart to seek them through…you can't see them with the eyes; the mind cannot come on this journey. Take yourself inside, and find the beauty that awaits you today, that is waiting for your conscious embrace, that is simply whispering or shouting, "Momo, come grant yourself this day!"

Our life is meant to be experienced: that is the only virtue of existence, to actually live it. We forget to do this almost always, getting caught up in the interpretation of life instead of in the observation of what it is. I know of a moment when you and I were immersed in what was and thus, in what is. We were walking towards the sunset on a very similar occasion to many before and many that followed. We loved doing this, you and I: walking together, crafting our "walks," walking side by side, always towards the sunset, reflecting on our day, on our smiles, on the lessons learned, and then watching how the sun gladly shared them and glared light back in appreciation. We did this at the beach. We walked together. Always. You and me, and love in between, with understanding and friendship and true brotherhood. We were crafting the way of the warrior, and we were teaching ourselves how to become that warrior. Well, today, use your heart as the guide and ask your feet to follow. The sun is glaring at you, and I'm walking right beside you. Feel the waves breaking in, look at my tanned face smiling back at you, and look at our minds cease as our hearts open. Let's walk, my brother—always. Let's walk together!

I love you with all my heart, and today, let me walk with you.

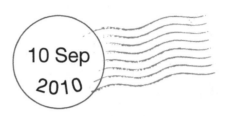

My dearest brother Momo,

I spoke with you mother and father last night, and a lot of peace flew to my heart, and I want to share it with you today. They spoke of a true warrior, of a candid spirit, of a son who for the first time in a long time was finally back: back in love, back with eyes full of light, back to the grace of life, because he saw it in himself first. We spoke of the beautiful letter you sent your mother and how she saw you for the first time after all the to and fro of not knowing how it might finally end. What they saw is what we all see, what we all know, how we all celebrate your life: a warrior poet! You are brilliant in every aspect, and this I know.

I mentioned to your mom that when you hit rock bottom, the only way is up. Now this is obviously relative, but in this point in your life, let's call this rock bottom, and let's ensure the fact that the only way is up. Let me offer a parallel insight: the only way to go when one wants to go up, is to go inside. Go inside, back to the root of the root of yourself, back to the innate glory. As she and I mentioned, this is a precious point in your life, a point in which there are no external stimuli competing for your attention, no false precepts obstructing your consciousness from connecting to yourself, and no distractions to keep you from one thing: listening to yourself and thus listening to the divine within, reconnecting to that power, that truth, that emblem of existential purity. Rest assured knowing that people suffer far more in prisons that have no bars. You are in a golden situation, one in which since the first moment, God's hand has shown itself to be ever present and strong. Take a hold of that hand and remember…simply ask yourself to listen and then let the magic flow on its own.

I love you with all my heart, and today, let me walk with you.

My dearest brother Momo,

In my past email, I mentioned coming back to the root of the root of yourself. The message comes from Rumi, a brilliant Sufi poet that shared his wisdom with us many years ago. Today I want to share with you the essence of that poem, so it might walk with you too, any day of your choosing.

The poem's essence is a loving call to action to come back, courageously and continuously, to the essence of our essence. It is there, at the core and very root of our existential expression, where we can reclaim our treasure chest of strength and love and be cradled by a space free of ego, doubt, fear, and sadness.

Just as the poem says, remember not to fix your eyes too low, for we are all God's children. A worthy existential enterprise that connects to the art of LIVING WHAT IS is to choose, consciously, to focus on the beautiful aspects of your everyday life: your girlfriend, the transcendentally communal love of all the people who know you, your friends, your past experiences as memories, your truth, your thoughts, your family, and everything in between. That is all there because of you, for you, next to you. It's all there. And we're all here. And we share that always; we share the fact that we love you!

Go now with a smile to the root of the root of yourself. Your treasure awaits in the midst of all who love you. It is yours for life and can never be taken away.

I love you with all my heart, and today, let me walk with you.

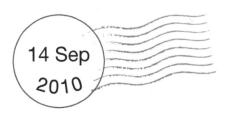

14 Sep
2010

My dearest brother Momo,

I'm getting prepared for a wicked and massive weekend here in the city… Mexico is turning 200 years old regarding its independence, and so the "scream" this time around will be amazing. Not sure what I'll be up to quite yet, but I'll surely be partying for 200 years worth of precious Mexican independence somewhere. I'll be thinking of you, my brother, and celebrating your nationality as well! Momo, I hope you have been able to find me walking next to you in the hallway and that you can see the sun reflected on my face day in and day out, just as it was during our walks on the beach. I truly hope so, because I am there, because everything that we have lived is there, and because there is absolutely no other way. I hope you are also remembering how to use your heart to see rightly, to find the essential beauty in everything, because we are all connected by the same token of appreciation: consciousness, the acknowledgment of that which is!

I'm going to share with you something that I'm so happy about right now, because I know as a fellow tripper and worthy musician, you will internalize the worth. I have bought the following concert tickets to go see with my girlfriend; there may be too many, and they are all starting in two weeks: Spoon, Interpol, James, Pixies, Air, Hot Chip, Faithless, and Arcade Fire. Wow! I know you can feel that. And guess what? You'll be jamming right next to me, Momo, feeling those virtuous souls elevate ours with their music, their presence, and their overall being. And quite frankly, I see yourself doing exactly the same thing…in due time it will become strong and obvious, but I know it is already happening, it's already there. Anyone who has the virtue of being near you will immediately recognize that there is something precious there, that there is something they can learn from, that there is something they can appreciate. And you will become that beacon of light, because you will have found it in yourself. And those who shine a light cannot keep it from themselves; on the contrary, it is because they see it that they realize that they can only share it, only fuel its fire, and only enjoy its presence. That's you. Whether you're ready to face it or not. You are a luminous being, and the light will shine deep and true. Shine it and reflect it!

I love you with all my heart, and today, let me walk with you.

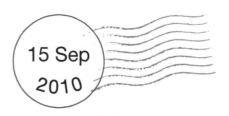

15 Sep
2010

My dearest brother Momo,

I'm sitting at the cubicle now getting ready for the national festivities. Two hundred years of independence...those are a lot of years of Mexicans being Mexican...lot's to celebrate, lots to indulge in, lots to commemorate. I want to come back to the notion I had explained earlier on that many people find themselves in far worse prisons that have no bars, because I think its worthy of further depth, for through its contrast, we can learn to appreciate a little bit of everything. You think about the great ones, and most have had a serious time in their life of epic tribulations...many of whom share your same situation: incarceration for unjust means or similar causes. Many, many come to mind: Mandela, the Hurricane, really and truly honest people, exemplary human beings that in some way or another felt they needed to experience something like this (for they weren't victims and knew it) and decided to focus on the treasure of the experience. They knew that it was exactly in the process of experiencing just that that they would allow themselves the virtue of learning from it.

As I mentioned before, I really do see this as a blessing, because as a human race we are terrible at listening to ourselves; we are so caught up in being existential escape artists, existential Houdinis, swinging from one external stimuli to the next, keeping everything at surface area and not going deeper, being terrified of the depths of ourselves because of our innate vulnerability, because of having to feel, because of having to connect, and because of having to acknowledge that the process is real, present, and all-consuming. That is why people live in far worse prisons, because the bars they erect are the ones keeping them from themselves, keeping them from connecting to themselves, keeping them from their own truth. These existential escape artists, as we all are at times inevitably so, fail to do the two things we need to do: to live and to be human, to experiment, feel, and observe ourselves doing all of these things at once. What is there to lose? Absolutely everything, for in our life lies the possibility of experiencing all human conditions and experiences… it's simply that fascinating. In the space between two individuals lies the space for all to be lived and experienced.

The world lives within us. So your current situation fuels this scenario and epitomizes the virtue of re-connecting, of knocking down the bars that keep you from yourself. The treasure is a true existential elixir. Thank yourself for having the balls to give you the opportunity to find yourself again! Again, remember proudly how you are the warrior poet, slowly but surely crafting that space for reconnecting from where you will, just as the great ones, join the movement towards unity and consciousness as a leader, as a re-united individual, and as a warrior!

I love you with all my heart, and today, let me walk with you.

My dearest brother Momo,

I hope you had an excellent weekend. The context doesn't matter, a weekend is a weekend, and I hope you had a beautiful one. Mine was full of a little bit of everything…a lot of celebration for independence (ergo my silence for a few days, for which I do apologize, as I left the city), a lot of love with my girlfriend (which I will tell you about in subsequent emails, as that story deserves its space and time), a lot of drinking and reminiscing and simply connecting. I feel just like all Mondays, a little blue and a little self-conscious as well, slowly getting over the "lump" of treating yourself so poorly over the weekend…which is actually something I wanted to share with you, a reflection that I am willing to share, because it connects with your current situation as well, for it has the same purpose.

I want to re-connect to myself and listen a bit more, to find that space to retreat into the root of the root of myself again. The weekend is so profound, so crazy, so dissonant to my week that it rids me of any sense of emotional stability when I'm cruising the 9-5 daily job. It takes a huge toll on me—the weekend—because I simply devour myself in bouts of hedonistic endeavors: drinking, partying, and really and truly living. It's beautiful, it's so powerful, but at the same time, it's simply so dissonant…I want to stop living at the extremes…no more white being the week and black being the weekend…I need to allow myself to trip the gray area, to be ok with something not being epic, to somehow allow myself to simply be there and not have to lose myself to find myself over the weekend…I am such a fan of living, though, that it is hard for me to not want to dance that night away, to feel everything sinking deep into me because it's so vivid and present. But that's a state of mind; that's simply a pre-conceived notion of something I am set on already experiencing and not necessarily the experience itself. But anyways, those are my reflections from the Monday cubicle blues.

I want you to know that I have made a decision to get back to the root of the root of myself just like you, and I will get it done. It's a process no doubt, a beautiful voyage, and it never ends, oh no, it never ends, but few ever start. The relationship with ourselves is the only relationship that needs tending, for it is the source of all the rest, and it is the recognition of the innate divinity we all share. If we pay attention to that, if we collaborate with the universe to find that, then we will always cherish the known and thus allow ourselves to share our truth with love. That's where it's at! Until tomorrow, my dear brother, big hug and lots of love!

I love you with all my heart, and today, let me walk with you!

22 Sep
2010

My dearest brother Momo,

I would like to share with you a little bit of transcendental philosophy today. It's heavy, but then again, as Dostoevsky said, "Suffering is the origin of consciousness." What I offer is what the philosopher I will talk about wanted to offer: freedom and empowerment, the opportunity to become who you are. This brilliant, misunderstood soul was none other than Nietzsche. The point is not to suffer, not by a long shot; the point is to reconnect, to re-examine, and to re-author a new choice on how to a) perceive any given situation (from the inside out) and b) how to channel that perception to accomplish something of power, truth, and meaning to you. This guy's theory is called "Eternal Recurrence."

I will spare you the metaphysical details regarding the premise behind the theory, but it's enough to say that it's based on the notion that time is infinite, but the space in which we inhabit is finite. Therefore, everything that is being lived now has to have already been lived, and the same goes for the future. Consequently, every present moment has the potential, and in his words this is definitely the case, to be re-lived, to recur eternally, from past to present and from present to future. That was the physics aspect of it; now let's get into the existential portion of it, the crux of the matter: the breath of life and true force.

What Nietzsche offers is a thought experiment. Imagine that this premise was definitely true, and all of a sudden someone comes along and tells you this premise, and you, for once today, understand that the way you live your day has to be well thought out. You will live this day, exactly as you did, making the same choices that you did, harnessing the same feelings and emotions as you did, eternally. Therefore, this premise can liberate you completely by forcing you to ask yourself, "How would I live my every day; what would I choose to eat, feel, think, do, if I knew that I would have to re-live this day, exactly as I did today, eternally?" Or it can suffocate you by making you face the fact that if today you chose to harness negative emotions, if your attention is centered on doing harm rather than good, if you are tripping the dark side, then you will have to do this, in exactly the same way, always. So herein lies a very magical weapon of existential perspective that can grant us the ability to choose again, to re-author our commitment to our 24 hour life spans and choose accordingly, because everything we choose to see, do, and feel will be lived on in exactly the same way.

I invite you, my dear brother, to internalize this truth regardless of your present context and to seek the truly transcendental in every day, because it's there, it's everywhere, and it's for our honest appreciation. This connects to another one of his premises, in which he says, "You must learn how to die right." Now by this, he means that death comes only, and should come only, after you have consumed your life entirely: meaning that you have really, truly, deeply LIVED. Only a life well-lived can have a death well-died. Therefore he asks us to live accordingly, to consume our life, and thus leave death only to the very end, when there is no more life to be lived and the only other option is death.

There are too many people who die before they are buried, too many who give in and stop trying, because their eyes are fixed on the rational, on the third dimension...but you don't need eyes to see; you need vision. In the vision lies the inner transcendental truth, the divine power, the everything. It's fascinating when you rule your life based on the essential...everything magically curves into perfect harmony. It's fascinating, because it's pure and perfect, and because it is always like this.

My dear brother, take this inside you and recur eternally, with a smile, and consume your life entirely, so that that force is what resonates and recurs, until the death that awaits us all comes in a very far future... only after our smiles are still very present and resounding.

I love you with all my heart, and today, let me walk with you.

23 Sep
2010

My dearest brother Momo,

I hope you are having, or had, a fantastic day. I'm not sure when you actually get a chance to read my emails, but I like to think of them reaching you sometime in the morning, so that they may walk with you during the day, sharing in the love and the experience, for you know that I am happy to be there by your side. I don't know if I had mentioned this earlier, but I might have…in any case, I've learned in life that one of the greatest teachers, apart from experience, is the ability to experiment with, and to actually connect with, CONTRAST.

For me, contrast elucidates wisdom. It's that simple. Wisdom will be attained through contrast. How so? First off, you can see how powerful the concept of contrast is in the most basic of things: you will only fully know, fully connect with, and fully understand that someone is short only after you see them next to someone who is tall, and vice versa. It is that epic contrast that elucidates wisdom, in this case, wisdom as the recognition, the acknowledgment of truth, as a product of experience. That is why travelling, and travelling as far and distant from what we are accustomed to, proves so exhilarating and ultimately life changing. By travelling, we are throwing ourselves into an environment that is fundamentally and absolutely different from our own. Therefore many of the things, concepts, ideas, ways of acting, etc., that we took for granted, or at least grew deeply accustomed to, get a fresh perspective through contrast.

Nothing is ever the same. We therefore allow ourselves to change our own anticipated perspective on life itself, to draw new conclusions, to expand our mind. This brings me to the next point of human evolution and, in this case, the beautiful connection between the process of attaining wisdom through contrast and the actual biological and mental effect that this has…I'm not sure if you are familiar with a term called plasticity, but it refers to an amazing ability of our brain! Basically, our brain expands as a result of new experiences! Fascinating!

The Buddhist monks have caught onto this fairly quickly and now magnify the power of deep meditation, as it also fuels plasticity. So if new experiences expand our mind, literally expand it, and new experiences always grant contrast, then we are wiser through contrast. We have an expanded mind through experience, and thus we must rejoice in the presence of mind-altering, fundamentally changing, all-new, and all-encompassing experiences! My dear brother, I am writing this so that you will realize that you are living exactly this right now. You are living a life-altering ecosystem that will grant you new, contrasting, and virtuous experiences on a daily basis, each moment and every minute.

You have basically given yourself a very powerful existential gift, because some of us have to hop on the plane and plan the vacation; some of us have to really go out of our way and out of our comfort zone to find that contrast, to really find a new experience that will expand our mind, but all you have to do is open your eyes! You have a series of contrasting experiences waiting, all of which will sink into your brain as they expand it, little by little, so that your soul begins to encompass something of brilliance and of wisdom: a product of contrasting your past and present emotions, thoughts, premonitions, etc., and renegotiating them in terms of your all-encompassing new environment! You are living what many of us pay thousands to accomplish: a life-changing experience. That's exactly how you have to live it: by staying true to that source of plasticity, because when you break with an established order, you create new existential meaning.

That is why travelling, starting a business, or anything that is mildly existentially entrepreneurial is so damn intoxicating and real, because we are redefining the way we choose to live our own life! Congratulations, my brother, for not many have the balls to give themselves this gift and even fewer are conscious of it once it is there. Be conscious, be grateful, and enjoy the expansion of contrasting wisdom!

I love you with all my heart, and today, let me walk with you.

24 Sep
2010

My dearest brother Momo,

"Life's a garden—dig it." I just remembered that phrase from a movie called "Joe Dirt." It's mighty ridiculous yet wildly powerful. Life must be dug. I wanted to point something out, because I honestly have no idea at which point in time you actually receive these emails: if they come one at a time, or in bulk, or what the deal is. My intention, and what I have been assuming, is for you to receive an email every day, hopefully in the morning or even in the evening, so that it might be something of value to start your day or to end it. In any case, that's really beside the point; even if you receive them in bulk, I trust you will read them accordingly. You can read them out of sequence (for they follow no particular sequence) and read them just as you feel them. These are for you, and you are the gift intended.

I remembered something very simple the other day that goes a very long way, and I would like to share it with you. I'm not sure if you've seen it before, but a few years ago a PowerPoint presentation was sent around, and it was about people being asked what they thought the most important thing in life was, what was worth the most. Answers varied and included a little bit of everything: money, friendship, love, family, etc. A percentage point was then assigned to every letter in the alphabet: A being 1%, B being 2%, and so on, and then all the letters of all the different things listed were added up.

The point was to see which term, concept, idea, or thing added up to 100% and would thus prove, with that simple exercise, what might indeed be the most valuable asset in a life. Well, the answer wasn't money, friendship, or love; the answer was ATTITUDE. Add them up; they are 1-20-20-9-20-21-4-5 respectively, and it goes without saying that attitude definitely is the most valuable asset we have. Why? Because the attitude you harness will allow you to put the worth you want on anything. Therefore, with the right attitude, money is enough, your family is just perfect, your friends are exactly what you need, and everything occupies a very harmonious place in your life: a place you have assigned and accepted, a place that your attitude has learned to appreciate, behold, and encompass, and most importantly, a place that your attitude, and thus your heart, has learned to appreciate!

There is only one step further than appreciation and that is to be thankful. If we fuel an attitude in life in which we remain thankful, simply thankful, then not only have we sought out and identified the worth in everything because we have appreciated it, but we have also allowed it to carve a special place in our life, because we have granted it an open mind and heart by being thankful. Being thankful is an immediate and conscious decision that everything has innate worth. You can obviously be thankful for a poor situation, for something "bad" happening in your life, because it carves character, identity, emotion, etc. Once you have identified and acknowledged the virtue that it brings, you can be thankful for that bad thing.

Therefore, to be thankful is to acknowledge virtue as an automatic endeavor. What better attitude can there be than that? If I were asked what attitude I would like to practice and share, I would love to be able to answer, "I acknowledge virtue as an automatic endeavor. I am fixed on the innate worth of it all, and thus I live gratefully." Wow. There is such power in that phrase, such beautiful power. And that's exactly how we can live, if we choose so. It's the existential 100%. It's the holy grail of a constant smile. It's our call and responsibility as caring beings, and it's our right.

I love you with all of my heart, and today, let me walk with you.

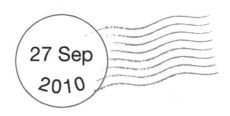

27 Sep
2010

My dearest brother Momo,

I would like to share with you this brief excerpt from Ken Wilbur's book *One Taste* that is magical and powerful, for it speaks about what we have been discussing—how to find the innate glory in everything, how to harness that attitude, and how to communicate it as an existential burden of hope. Enjoy!

From Ken Wilber, *One Taste:*

"And therefore, all of those for whom authentic transformation has deeply unseated their souls must, I believe, wrestle with the profound moral obligation to shout from the heart—perhaps quietly and gently, with tears of reluctance; perhaps with fierce fire and angry wisdom; perhaps with slow and careful analysis; perhaps by unshakable public example— but authenticity always and absolutely carries a demand and duty: you must speak out, to the best of your ability, and shake the spiritual tree, and shine your headlights into the eyes of the complacent.

You must let that radical realization rumble through your veins and rattle those around you.

Alas, if you fail to do so, you are betraying your own authenticity. You are hiding your true estate. You don't want to upset others because you don't want to upset yourself. You are acting in bad faith, the taste of bad infinity.

Because, you see, the alarming fact is that any realization of depth carries a terrible burden: those who are allowed to see are simultaneously saddled with the obligation to communicate it to others. And therefore, if you have seen, you simply must speak out. Speak out with compassion, or speak out with angry wisdom, or speak out with skillful means, but speak out you must.

And this is truly a terrible burden, a horrible burden, because in any case there is no room for timidity. The fact that you might be wrong is simply no excuse: You might be right in your communication, and you might be wrong, but that does not matter. What does matter, as Kierkegaard so rudely reminded us, is that only by investing and speaking your vision with passion, can the truth, one way or another, fully penetrate the reluctance of the world. If you are right, or if you are wrong, it is only your passion that will force either to be discovered. It is your duty to promote that discovery — either way— and therefore it is your duty to speak your truth with whatever passion and courage you can find in your heart. You must shout, in whatever way you can."

I love you with all my heart, and today, let me walk with you.

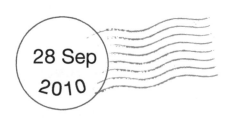

28 Sep
2010

My dearest brother Momo,

I hope you are well and that you have enjoyed your family's visit, which I think you received not too long ago. It must have been beautiful. I heard from your sister that you are receiving my emails, so that's fantastic, and worry not brother, there is absolutely no need for you to respond; just knowing that you are actually receiving them will suffice. I wanted to share with you a little bit more on perspective and contrast, but this time, on something regarding rhythm and pause as a state of wisdom and clarity....

I can only reflect on this via personal observation and mediation, as I have been going through the same process. Ever since I returned from Rwanda, and from Babson in general, I've been living a very different type of life here in Mexico. Certain elements are the same: I live on my own but with friends, I am self-sufficient; certain elements are new: I am in a serious relationship, I have a serious job, and things are simply mixed well. There is one key element, though, that has been missing since the beginning here, and that is the adrenaline fix, the thrill: the enormous and implacable sense of mastering things beyond my own control, of getting everything done in serious productivity mode, in short, of being intense and wildly injected into everything. That is how I lived for four years during college, and that is exactly how I lived in the social entrepreneurial scene in Rwanda.

Therefore, for the first time in a long time, I have rid myself of a main existential escape catalyst: adrenaline and intensity. For the first time in a long time, I am not SO caught up in absolutely everything, so immersed in every single aspect of life, that I actually get to savor every aspect of life, because its reality, its natural state, and its essence appear…and not my digested perception of it diluted with extreme passion, diligence, and just plain old productivity. What I'm trying to say, is that I have been granted a brand new opportunity to see myself, to get to know myself, and to re-connect with reality. I have had to come to terms with the "slow" times; I have had to allow myself what was once an inconceivable premise: to get bored.

I have experienced what it means not to fully love something, not to be fully passionate about something; what it means to have more of a "blah" day to day experience, travelling lightly and not having to be the leader, fully responsible, and always extra efficient. But what have I gotten as I excused myself from that overly stimulating environment? Me! I got myself back. I have had to greet reality (in all of its grays, whites, and blacks) face-to-face and redesign a theory of self-love and acceptance, because I can no longer escape through doing. And I am slowly coming to terms with how we are indeed human beings, not human doings. I have managed to bring to light all those aspects of my personality and all those unyielding emotional wounds that I had placed on the backburner because I "didn't have the time" back in the ultra productivity mode, and I have had to face them, listen to them, and finally heal them.

It hasn't been an easy process at all coming back to Mexico, because things are shifting, things are finding their space, and the dust is moving.

It always hurts the eyes when you step out of the movie theater and meet the glaring reality outside. My eyes are glaring…but they are open, and now I'm using the heart to see rightly, not the mind. It is turning out to be a magnificent process of re-discovery, all because the existential rhythm changed, because I allowed myself to experience whatever this is fully, without fear, and with an open heart. It is in this space of contrast that I grant myself the opportunity to become and to heal. Now I share this with you, because you find yourself in a very similar position. Fortunately though, your degree of minimization of external stimuli is much grander than mine, making thus, at the same time, the space for personal connection, healing, inquiry, and consciousness much larger.

This is all a part of your choosing, that is the opportunity to reconnect, and you must embrace its magical power, as your soul was hungry for this experience. Imagine the world we would live in if people granted themselves the opportunity of self-love, self-knowledge, self-healing: in short, if they allowed themselves the existential silence needed to finally listen? We would be hugging each other a lot more, we would be stopping on the side of the road to greet one another more often, and we would be focused on the shedding of light instead of on its absence. This is the space of becoming, my brother, for all else is quieting in order for you to listen. You, however, are speaking. Connect to that voice and immerse in its truth. It needs the audience.

I love you with all my heart, and today, let me walk with you.

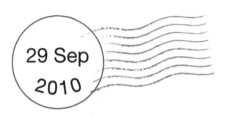

29 Sep
2010

My dearest brother Momo,

I received an email from your mom today saying that she had seen you and that you had light in your eyes, love in your heart, and a big smile. This makes me feel so amazing; you have no idea. You are a true alchemist, my brother, grinding every situation into existential gold, making it virtuous and awesome, and for that you must salute yourself day in and day out! I truly envy your situation in a very unique manner, and it's parallel to what I wrote about yesterday: the power behind granting ourselves that opportunity for existential silence, so that we can finally begin to listen.

I keep on thinking about it, and the truth is ever clearer. When we quiet the outside, the inside becomes audible: it's really that simple. We have indeed trained ourselves to remain at the surface level; there are far too many external stimuli competing for our attention, and thus we fail to go deeper, fail to take things to a deeper level of internalization and consciousness, and so we have become existential escape artists, existential Houdinis.... What ends up happening is that we lose sight of ourselves and forget that voice that lives within, the divine voice, the voice of the ages, and the purity in everything.

When we turn our focus inside, the things we had forgotten or failed to pay attention to begin to take form and claim their power. Things such as forgiveness, true peace, freedom, silence, faith, health, and tranquility…ease of mind…ease of character…and centered focus. It is therefore imperative and worthwhile to grant ourselves these moments and to appreciate when life itself throws us these golden opportunities to turn, face the mirror, and begin reflecting our inner light. This time, you have an opportunity to create new habits: habits that include listening and centering your light and attention and habits for understanding that all perspective comes from within, that your thoughts and intentions govern absolutely every movement in this universe, that our world is one of endless possibility that is at our fingertips simply because we exist. It is an existential training session that will help you transcend any experience, for you will forever remember that the only truth is the one inside you; it is the one inside us all, and if you connect to that truth and use it as the source to fuel all perspectives, then that is heaven on earth in every instance, that is just harmony, and that just is…both good and bad, just everything, simply there.

I love you with all my heart, and today, let me walk with you.

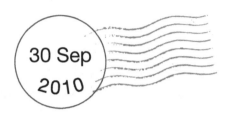

30 Sep
2010

My dearest brother Momo,

The first part of my message is a message from my sister, Mariana, who
wanted me to forward some words: "Love you Momo, hang in there and
stay close to God, for he will give you strength to overcome this situation
and keep you strong for the aftermath. I pray for you and love you very
much, Mariana." I wanted to comment a little today on the power of
intention, for it definitely plays a role in your current situation, regarding
your immediate goals and objectives, and in all aspects of life.

The premise is beautifully simple, but its power and the realization of
its proper execution is what grants eternal freedom…and responsibility—
conscious responsibility. The premise is that our external world mirrors
our internal world perfectly! That means that our internal environment,
composed of thoughts, emotions, and any degree of existential attention,
will create our external world. There is absolute perfect harmony in this
endeavor, and it is our human maxim.

The problem, and why we choose to ignore and forget this simple
truth, is a) who wants to have full responsibility over their life and

world? People love to escape "guilt," love to be able to point the finger, and no one chooses to hold themselves completely accountable. and b) most of the things that we harbor, we maintain at an unconscious level. This supports reason a), for if we don't know it (or so we tell ourselves), then how could we ever blame ourselves for causing just that? Those are the grand tricks we play on ourselves; the problem is that we actually believe we are fortunate enough to dupe ourselves. There is a consciousness reservoir in our soul, a place where all of these thoughts and emotions are being ticked, tallied, summed, and kept on file, and their conscious acknowledgment surges at due time...it always does. Thus they come out and play, just as they should, in our external world, and we either experience them and learn, or they come back and back again...or they cling into the internal sphere, slowly infecting the source of other thoughts and emotions, until we choose to bring them to light and pay attention...and listen. So, wherein lies the power of intention? Intention is none other than the space to which we direct our attention and attention is energy and energy is our self, our internal world, channeled through to attain a purpose. There is one key element for an intention, which is our internal conscious conviction of an external outcome: to become visible and present, just as the rule claims. It has to be honest.

Therein lie the consciousness factor and the responsibility factor. We have to know, in our own hearts, why we want that which we claim we want, why we desire that outcome, why we would like to see that take place. And we need to hold ourselves accountable through honesty. There is no right or wrong conviction, they simply have to be brought to light unfiltered and faced honestly. When that happens, you connect to that intention in a very profound way: in the only way needed for that conviction to actually play out its role in the external arena. You will feel the intention deep inside you, because you have accepted yourself and channeled that part of yourself into the realization of that endeavor.

So we can't simply think about something and consider it done; we must feel that something, feel it truly and honestly, and dedicate ourselves toward channeling that conscious energy into first visualizing and then trusting (God) for its harmonious execution, if that's what will ring valuable to our lives in that present context. This exercise of intention will help you in absolutely anything, for you will know a) you have absolute responsibility and power over your external circumstances and b) how to magnify that power and inject yourself into any endeavor, so that it happens if it actually needs to. You've done your part, you've channeled yourself. You are there. Well, my dear brother, I'm off to the weekend, and I send you massive hugs to be with you. Channel yourself and simply sit back and enjoy the realization of it!

I love you with all my heart, and today, let me walk with you.

Part II
October 2010

*Experience is not what happens
to you; it's what you do with
what happens to you*
Aldous Huxley

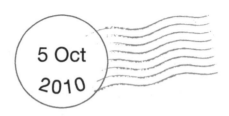

5 Oct
2010

My dearest brother Momo,

I hope the sun came up nice and bright for you today, my brother! I wanted to share with you a little bit regarding the inner versus the outer world. We've already talked about how they are indeed one and the same: how there is perfect harmony in the harboring of internal, honest intentions and their external execution. Perfect harmony.

What I wanted to touch on today is the truth of your internal world and how it isn't up for grabs. I mention this because it is very difficult at times, and more so when immersed in very contrasting contexts or situations, to stay true to our internal convictions, our internal reality. It's not necessarily that we sway, lose sight of it, or forget it, but it's that we place it up for grabs; we forget its cemented worth of being our internal world, and thus we open it up for a conversation, a negotiation with the external world. This can happen when we feel alone, when we feel we don't belong, but most of the time it happens when we feel misunderstood or when we think we are the only ones mastering this internal dialogue, the only ones actually reading the fine print, the only ones in the movie theater. And so in comes a deadly friend called DOUBT, and we begin to question that which needs no questioning, that which is built on the acceptance of faith and love and the knowledge that everything is as it should be. As you can see, when we place our attention on the outside world, on the external validation of our internal context, that's when the deadly friend kicks in.

The way of the warrior poet is to seek the internal validation of your external world: to force the external world to come from that inner validation, from that source of acceptance and acknowledgment. When the world is turning, when doubt peeps its head, when there is more noise than peace, then maybe we've let our mind take over and forgotten about simply experiencing…for remember we are human beings and not human doings, and some things are just meant to be experienced fully, for in that arena lies the ability to appreciate, to fully comprehend, to internalize, and thus to heal! So walk tall, my brother, and manifest your confident strides from the inside out. Trace your steps from the soul and from the heart and then follow them trustingly, knowing those are your steps and that they aren't up for grabs. Your only responsibility is to grant dignity, light, and acceptance to those steps.

I love you with all my heart, and today, let me walk with you.

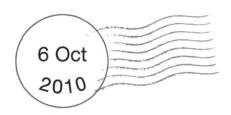

6 Oct
2010

My dearest brother Momo,

I just thought of something: Remember that guitar that we bought in Cuernavaca way back when? Do you remember that you had it for a while, then I had it for a while, and then we scribbled something on the front of it with the guitar pick? I would love to remember what it said. Do you remember? I can remember the guitar pick we used to scribble on it though…I think it was a short, fat, stubby, purple pick that we bought together. I loved that guitar, man. I still have it in my mind, remembering how I used it to serenade the deepest of loves, just as it was designed to. It's simply fantastic to harbor these beautiful memories, simply fantastic. I also remember—and this trip really is one of my all-time favorites, because it felt so good—that time that your family and mine travelled together in Spain. Remember playing beach tennis and making sure we would hit the ball close to hot girls, so that we could then see if they would help us throw the ball back? Man, that was precious!

Remember drinking beer with my sister on the curb? Remember your mom waking us up at 6:00 a.m. right after lighting a cigarette and the time our rented house got flooded? Can you re-inject those feelings, man? Remember having hookah and watching *"Friends"* back at your house for hours…and making mixed CDs and listening to them full throttle, as we cruised down the Côte d'Azur? These are the wonders of life, my brother, and the best thing is that they are just as good as our sunsets, for they are frozen there: they are internalized, and we have direct, free, and eternal access to them at anytime. These are the moments of our story, and they bring warmth, love, and too many smiles to my life—too many. There is only one thought that makes me happier in this context: the certainty that the moments to come will be infinitely better. Imagine the next sunset! Imagine the next curbside beer! Imagine the next, imagine the next, imagine the next. Well, guess what? It's already here. It lives within us forever, my dear brother, forever. That is our internal truth and mechanism, and just like the other ones, they aren't up for grabs. This is us, and we always have it. So much goodness, so much damn goodness. It's all there, my brother—each and every instant. Take a deep breath and internalize the entire spectrum. I'm right there with you!

I love you with all my heart, and today, let me walk with you.

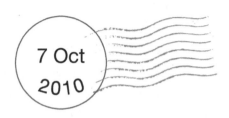

7 Oct
2010

My dearest brother Momo,

Just to continue with the comical nonsense of yesterday's email, I also thought I'd share these: you can try and picture me coming back from a wild night in Acapulco and apparently hurling myself into a flamingo that I was later charged fully for by a guilt-driven crusade of angry uncles and aunts who charged into our hotel room the next morning (much too early for guilt); or you taking a whiff of the piña colada scent on the beach and having to make an emergency face-first plunge into the nearest hole in order to hide the series of bad choices you had made the night before; or me stopping on my jet ski ride with my girlfriend to...well... appreciate the view...and having the dudes immediately come after me; or our dear uncle organizing a singing session with the hotel band on New Year's Eve to sing a little bit of "What Would Mary Say." Too good, man—totally amazing. And now on to the good stuff.

I was reading something the other day that definitely clarified many aspects of myself in terms of my perspective: how seeing what we see and living what we live are conscious decisions. And we can change those decisions every day of our lives. It had to do with a very simple message: treat and see everyone from a source of love. This is obviously much more easily said than done, especially after you have just had a confrontation with someone, or you see things that you don't like that much. However, the premise goes a little deeper, and it has to do with that attitude of gratefulness that I had touched upon earlier, and it takes it to a new level: to harbor an attitude of gracefulness and gratefulness and to be able to see and treat everyone from a source of love. How does it work? If we are grateful, you can remember that means that we have identified and acknowledged the worth of that situation, person, event, etc., in our life. So regardless of the current appreciation we have—even if we are caught up in emotion—if we can't really stand that person or situation in that moment or if we remind ourselves that their presence means perfect harmony in our life and is thus something to be grateful about, then immediately we are able to switch that essence of rejection to an essence of love.

The switch is that easy; it's recognizing the immediate worth of the person or situation, in the entirety of their context and self-worth (meaning we don't change or want to change them), and then allowing it to invade our life with a sense of purpose and meaning, of existential significance, that we can then use to fuel a source of love. Instead of saying, "I just can't stand that person, situation, event, etc.," we can now say, "Maybe I don't understand that person, but I am grateful for her presence in my life, for it is perfect, divine will, and valuable. I accept that person and the situation, and now I choose to choose again!"

This mechanism also breeds massive amounts of freedom, for we no longer tie ourselves down to the experience or situation or person; we simply understand that in order to be grateful, we must first accept what is there. Once we accept it, we let it go, we ALLOW it, and in the allowance, the magic of that interaction happens and continues to breathe life into our present state. I think that this is a wonderful way to see our lives, for it grants that freedom, and most importantly, it allows us to consciously and honestly choose to see everyone and everything through love. This does not mean we fail to see the reality—not at all— we call things by their right name, but we also accept them for what they are and remain thankful, conscious, and loving of their presence, for it adds existential value. This is a fantastic endeavor that we must train ourselves to rejoice in.

I love you with all my heart, and today, let me walk with you.

8 Oct
2010

My dearest brother Momo,

I wanted to remind you that what I wrote about yesterday is definitely easier said than done…but I also wanted to emphasize that it's completely possible and that the effects of implementing that attitude, of recognizing that worth, and of choosing to see the love, are major and beneficial. I know this because I did this yesterday. After writing the email, I made a conscious choice to practice exactly what I had written to you, and out came a bundle of fantastic experiences. What did I do in palpable terms? I opened up, I accepted, and I gave thanks.

That's it. I simply connected to that which was and asked the mind to take a hike and search for someone else to bother with ungrounded beliefs, thoughts, and expectations. It was beautiful, and so I just wanted to remind you that it is there and that it is powerfully possible, so very possible. To further comment on the experience, I think that what I achieved from that practice –from choosing to appreciate, to be graceful, to be grateful, and to magnify the love essence in all—is that I granted myself peace and tranquility. I am not fighting the person or the situation anymore, I'm not trying to change it, nor am I fixed on even understanding it. I am now focused on experiencing it, on connecting to its natural source without anything being sieved out. Thus I am freer and more relaxed, and when that happens, my vibration frequency and energy are also more relaxed, more poised, more open, and more trusting, which all serves as an invitational force for others vibrating at the same frequency to connect and share.

That's the actual beauty of these endeavors: they are completely self-nurturing, and they propagate themselves as we recognize and are attracted to that which we see in ourselves. That's the universal premise of "like with like," of people attracting that which they lack but also that which they recognize, so that together they can elevate each other in fruitful waves of connection. It's a fantastic process once you begin to see your vibration change, and you recognize that there is now something else oozing from you: something different and something altogether new and beautiful. We have to begin to harvest these internal conversations and support them with their due share of recognition and awareness. This is really a beautiful process, and it begins the moment we decide to make a difference, to allow ourselves to choose again, and to see that light in everything THROUGH ACCEPTANCE. To see innate value in others, one must first see it in oneself. Thus if you are recognizing innate value in others and being consciously appreciative of the situation, then that means you have first pronounced this on yourself. Use that as the guiding light and the reassurance of your innate value. You are you now: the warrior poet!

I love you with all my heart, and today, let me walk with you.

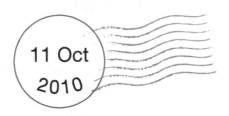

11 Oct 2010

My dearest brother Momo,

"Say goodbye, allow the river of life to flow, washing away the waters that you see, so that you can see those that are before you that you haven't yet seen, and the ones that are yet to come...." I was just sent this little excerpt in an email, and I thought I would share it with you. It speaks of endless virtue, when you realize that the easiest way to live life is to make a conscious effort to experience life...to let it flow just as it needs to, with the utmost faith and realization that *everything is as it should be.* If we do that, we are then able to say goodbye to the things that are holding us back from the present moment.

Nothing is for certain in this life, nothing holds itself permanently, and so learning how to say goodbye, with a smile on your face, is essential towards learning how to live. Saying goodbye allows the river to flow and, what's more, to bring in the new tide of hope, virtue, love, reality, and consciousness that desires to be properly internalized through acceptance. In this new context of yours, there are too many things you can say goodbye to, too many things. And that, if you follow the excerpt, is freedom redefined, because that means that your present context is granting you the parallel opportunity to receive many new tides and many new waters as you say goodbye to the old ones. If you choose to see with the heart in this new environment, you will magnify the truth of the new tide and connect to its infinite source of wisdom. The new tide will show you that you deserve absolutely everything, just by being alive.

If you make a decision now, in your heart, to accept this paramount headliner, then you will see the magic flow into your life. The era of wanting, of needing, of not deserving is fully over. In comes a brand new tide of fruitful possibility, one that only needs your conscious acknowledgment and conviction in order to flourish. Whatever you envision, whatever you choose to see, see it as done, give thanks for it as if it has already happened, and then you will see it happen just like that. You must, through your heart, acknowledge that your external world will reflect your internal world perfectly. Choose abundance and rid yourself of all negative thoughts. Make this your new river and ride it with a smile. Choose abundance through your heart's acknowledgment, and invite the perfection of your current context into your heart.

I love you with all my heart, and today, let me walk with you.

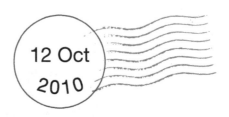

12 Oct
2010

My dearest brother Momo,

I'm going to share with you a recent reflection of mine that came to me as I thought about my different emotional states during these last few days. Basically, my realization is that I am addicted to adrenaline, to existential adrenaline, to the existential high. How do I get it? I can find it in too many ways but mostly, I think for me, it means to be caught up in something, to be intellectually and emotionally immersed into an endeavor, to be moved to the point of ecstasy and empowerment and to the point of feeling, simply, very alive. Now this is a state I have been harvesting for many years, and I only now have come to terms with the acceptance and realization that it has been the motor that drives many of my initiatives: both productive and not. It's quite ironic to believe that such a mechanism could give birth to unproductive outcomes, but just as with any addiction, one must keep it in check.

The reason for this is the same reason that applies to all addictions: when you don't have your usual fix, you lose your mind and possibly end up doing things you could have easily avoided if you had taken the time to breathe, to reflect, and to connect. So in practical terms, and for the first time in my life, I am not surrounded by an existential, all-too-thrilling, and awe-inspiring environment. I have a pretty okay life in general terms but nothing to scream at the top of my lungs about, nothing incredible, as it has been in the past. This is something new that I needed to experiment and live. I needed to understand the duller moments in life and, what's more, learn how to give myself the existential significance and thrill of an incredible life within a not-so-incredible life.

I must then become my own unremitting source of existential significance. Because my life now is more "okay" than it is "incredible," I get bored and miss the adrenaline rush: that feeling of riding the existential wave so high and so fast that a constant smile is the only thing I can manage to wear. What I realized, and where I have to be cautious, is to understand what happens when I get bored. What do I do to get that extra adrenaline fix in order to feel more alive?

I end up creating situations, events, things in my mind that are so complex and downright irksome that they compel me to think, to feel, to get overly agitated, to sink down, and jump up. In short, they force me to recreate the battlefront of those existentially thrilling moments. The only catch is that these "things" I create are not always positive; they are more often than not negative, and they turn into issues and problems because of their innate capacity to fuel my intellect, and thus I end up potentially suffering.

At the end of the day, the joke is on me, and it's a bad joke: a joke that could easily be avoided if I simply breathe, reflect, connect, and realize that what I am seeking for, I can easily give myself from the inside out. So, this is where I open the conversation up to illuminate your current context. Because you are also in a "duller" context (even though only in some ways is it duller, in other ways it is much more visceral and real, for the context of this conversation let's assume it's duller), you might have more time on your hands, more time to do nothing, fewer exhilarating objectives or projects, maybe fewer stimulating conversations, etc., and so you have the amazing opportunity to become that internal source of recurring existential stimulation that will guide and re-ignite any wave of existential high you might need. That being said, you will learn how to practice and cherish the art of not having to a) seek external validation for your existential high through exhilarating objectives or projects just for the sake of it and, more importantly, b) you will not have to get yourself into trouble or seek issues or create problems simply because you are bored or need a little extra adrenaline fix to feel more alive.

This is the real clinger, man, the real quintessence of freedom, because through the realization of this principle, you will be able to simply give yourself the doses that you need: the productive doses you need to simply know that you, just like everything else, are just as you should be. You will then catch yourself thinking these thoughts and be able to stop any potentially negative action before it happens by simply acknowledging that you were bored, that you needed to feel that existential edge again.

This is a battle for me, my brother, and I extend its acknowledgment to you, so that you may choose again, choose differently, and not have to fall into the traps of the existential addict, clinging for another dose of adrenaline rush. Use your current situation as a training ground and inject yourself through your own self every single day. Learn how to become the highest state of the existential wave BY SIMPLY LIVING, and learn how not to make yourself dependent on external actions and stimuli. This is key, my brother, and I salute you for having the place to practice!

I love you with all my heart, and today, let me walk with you.

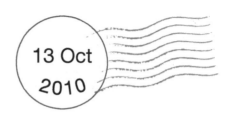

My dearest brother Momo,

I have a beautiful thing to share with you: I am just about to head off to see Arcade Fire live in Mexico. I will rejoice and enjoy this concert as if you were standing right next to me, man. It will be epic, and it will be profound. So just be aware of any extreme amount of energy you might be receiving shortly, for it will be me channeling their beautiful music all the way to you, my brother. I wanted to keep on commenting on what I brought up yesterday regarding the feeling bored and moving just to get that extra fix of life. I want to clarify that maybe there is another way to look at this.

Thus I offer a subtle, but very profound, difference. If we change our mindset and see it not as being "bored" but as "evolving"—that is, as a response to an inner urge to reach higher existential phenomena because the space we currently inhabit has already been sucked to the bone, then we can see more positive reflections arise. I prefer this view: we are pushed to move, pushed to reach higher, because we are fueled by an inner realization of a constant need for evolution, for higher significance.

That is why we cannot remain dull or mellow; we must continuously seek and move, because we are responding to a constant inner evolutionary agenda. So what happens now, is that we must frame all of this in terms of "evolutionary growth." Thus that adrenaline fix, that need to *transcend*, is the little bug called "evolutionary growth" eating away at us. So the question becomes, "What is next on my evolutionary agenda?" If you listen carefully to that bug and understand where we are and why the movement is happening (aka where do we want to be), then we will be able to clarify what is next on our evolutionary agenda, where that inner soul wants to be, and most importantly, why and with what effect. So what's next on your personal evolution? In your relationship with yourself? In the relationship with your surroundings? In the thought processes and feelings that harbor them?

This dialogue will allow us to connect to that power of wanting the extra fix by anticipating its presence and by choosing to roll with it. That way we can ask ourselves, "What can I do every day, in a different way, so that I can continue to evolve?" We are in a state of constant change and evolution; that much is certain. Thus when we feel that bug, that pinch, it is best to ask ourselves, "What's next?" "What is calling me now?" In that way, we can design a profitable path to accomplish just that and not remain unconscious of the inner push, of the evolutionary agenda, of that fantastic and all-encompassing breath of life!!!

I love you with all my heart, and today, let me walk with you.

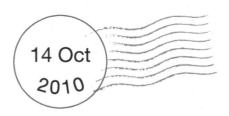

14 Oct
2010

My dearest brother Momo,

Arcade Fire was outstanding yesterday. I'm not sure if you are very familiar with the band, but it's simply hard to see a band these days that is completely immersed in their music, in the message they share, and in the love they set out to generate. They were the epitome of eclectic. It was just sublime, with everyone participating, everyone playing a different instrument, so caught up within themselves that you could feel every note, could really feel it was playing just for you, just that once, just in that way. Transcendental stuff, man; truly beautiful. I can clearly see why it is you chose to study music…what it means to allow yourself to be connected to that force, that truth, that beauty, and that power, all the time. It's such a wonderful channel and opportunity to reach people.

Throughout the entire concert, those guys had the attention of every single person in the stadium. They had not only the undivided attention of thousands, but the personal conviction, the determination of thousands to really live that moment to the maximum, to drift off, and to dream through the lyrics. The gift of music is the emotional and very human loyalty of all subjects, how they choose to connect, from the inside out, and to live within that moment. Nothing is more powerful than an army of loyal fans. They need to feel, and thus they will share the divinity of those beats with all.

There is a lot of movement in a concert, a lot of energy, but inside there is also peace, and there is the certainty that, for that moment, something rings true, something is beautiful, and there is perfection in that, absolute perfection. I think that it is grand of you to have committed to that transcendence. It can't be easy, as no emotional output highway is ever properly paved or without its due obstacles, but through music, one can always grant oneself the certainty of connection, of immediate loyalty, of an army of love. We can be anything in this world and very good at very different things, but even presidents come back to themselves through music.

We all allow ourselves the gift of ourselves through music. When, as an artist, you harbor this truth and fuel its power, you are giving everyone what they are always trying to find: a piece of themselves. Ahhhhh, what a sublime endeavor. What a calling, and what a life: the life of the conscious artist. I salute you, my dear brother, for you are exactly that!

I love you with all my heart, and today, let me walk with you.

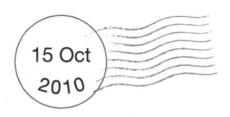

15 Oct
2010

My dearest brother Momo,

I wanted to share with you something I picked up from an email about psychology that landed in my inbox today. Basically, the notion is a beautiful relationship between the heart and the mind: specifically, what the heart wants to feel, the mind ends up creating and showing. Thus you can see how beautifully connected your emotional state is to the "reality" you choose to perceive or that which your mind shows you as a constant reality. The article goes in depth about psychoanalytic references to support the claims, but one of the most important studies shows that the way we speak to ourselves, because it has a serious effect on our emotions, will end up having a serious effect on our reality, on how we live. When you come to terms with this fact, you realize immediately that not only do you control your brain, but you also control your entire spectrum of reality, just by choosing to link proper emotions with their adequate realization through thought.

What is the best way to see which emotion we are triggering? Through speaking to ourselves. Why? Because in that dialogue, in that thought process, lies the channeling of those emotions into reality. Therefore, if you choose to speak to yourself with love, attention, kindness, and support, without ridding yourself of the grasp of reality, then you are allowing yourself to co-create that reality along with your thoughts...and then you will live it.

It's actually quite liberating when you think about it, because when you come face-to-face with a situation and all of the sudden it's going just as you expected, or it feels just as you expected it to, then you know that you can actually trace that reality back to a thought and that thought back to an emotion that was consciously or subconsciously designed to manifest itself all the way back to that present moment. I can see this play out in my life constantly, and then we still manage to lie to ourselves and try to find someone else or something else to blame. It's ridiculous once we know that we were owners all the time, authors of our reality, in full control of our present situation.

It's really quite fascinating, and I will practice this art of consciously trying to tag positive emotions and see them through to their momentary realization. I will also speak to myself accordingly, so that I can fuel that state and immerse myself within the power generated. This is a very valuable exercise and a very opportune insight for us to cherish.

I love you with all my heart, and today, let me walk with you.

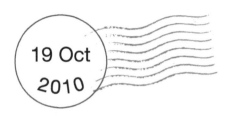

19 Oct
2010

My dearest brother Momo,

I feel you very close, my brother, and I love writing to you precisely for that reason! I kept reading yesterday on the power to create your reality, and the actual ownership we have over every single emotion, thought, and sentiment we channel. One of the main arguments was to recall, first of all, our innate divine nature.

Now if you extend from that realization, then you must comprehend that if your "spiritual" self wills it by visualizing it in the prefrontal cortex (this is the part of the brain where all the magic happens), then it is already a reality. However, since we are always attached to bodily cravings and to these "proofs" of the physical 3D world, then our mind doesn't allow us to genuinely believe it, and thus the "physical" self continues to will it…waiting for the proof, remaining skeptical, believing just enough to not believe…and to not believe because we think we don't deserve it. However, if you will it from the spiritual arena, have an honestly profound conviction that it is so, and visualize it accordingly in the prefrontal cortex, then it is

61

yours—all of it—but you have to feel it. It is truly powerful to grant ourselves this freedom and this power to orchestrate and define each and every one of our situations.

The same goes for those "unconscious" desires that somehow we believed would end up as a very palpable scene in our life. Everything is thus as it should be, and there is perfect harmony in that: perfect peace and order. We forget that we willed it, spiritually or physically, consciously or unconsciously; we had a conviction, and what we are living is a perfect representation of those intentions and things that we funneled through. Perfect harmony, order, and balance. Therefore we are not victims of circumstance. We cannot claim, "we didn't know." We cannot grant ourselves the privilege of remaining ignorant, of saying, "but I thought it would be different." If we take enough time to dig deeply enough, then we can unmask our true intentions, bring them out of the unconscious sphere, and negotiate their validity in the conscious sphere. We should give ourselves this right, for we hid these intentions deep in our chest, and we must be courageous enough to face them internally before we face them in the external reality. If we still will them, then so be it, but what if we can change them?

What if we can revisit them and negotiate their truth? What if we can ask ourselves, "What do we really, honestly and really, want?" What would be easier? Would it be easier to acknowledge that we secretly hoped for failure, because it might give us a tempting chance to feel sorry for ourselves? Or did we hope for failure, because we sincerely believe we don't deserve the success? Or do we simply want a "less than optimal" scenario, so that we can simply find a more optimal scenario in something else and thus even out the score? Remember that we are constantly seeking pain, because we believe that only from a state of pain can we first seek and then find pleasure. How ironic, right? We continually chastise ourselves and force ourselves to fail, because we need the pain to then seek the pleasure.

We forget that we own every ounce of pleasure that we could possibly endure if we want to claim the right of ownership. Thus, once we remember that our pleasure is ours to give and receive, we can then do without the pain and simply stick to the pleasure principle. That way there is no need to fail, no need to suffer; there is only the absolute realization that we WANT TO CHOOSE AGAIN, and that we choose to will our pleasure spiritually, that we choose life and love and endless possibility, that we own our right to claim what we need and want, and that we can do this ALWAYS. I am on the path of granting myself the possibility to always choose again and to acknowledge my freedom and innate ability to grant myself pleasure without the previous experience of suffering and pain. Let's hold our hands in this endeavor, my brother!

I love you with all my heart, and today, let me walk with you.

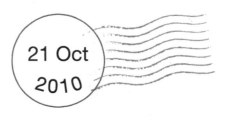

My dearest brother Momo,

I wanted to share with you something that I practiced this morning that really did work, and it has to do with the projection of the prefrontal cortex and the ability to actually visualize and truly believe that what you indeed desire will happen just by virtue of you desiring it honestly. There is one thing I had forgotten to mention and that is the difference between the objective, conscious mind and the subconscious mind.

The reality of the matter is that we have to allow ourselves the virtue of bridging both, of reconciling both, in order to really project onto reality our innermost desires. Why must they be reconciled? It is because our subconscious mind is used to sabotaging us via numerous mechanisms. Since it is subconscious, the games it plays remain fairly unnoticed, yet their power is just as strong because, conscious or not, we have willed their presence. The subconscious mind holds those emotions of self-boycott and guilt—the ones that do not allow us to fully feel that we deserve the thing we desire—but most importantly, it holds the inner reminder of the past. The past should never be taken into consideration once we project ourselves into the future or cling to the created image in the prefrontal cortex of that which we desire.

The past doesn't exist, as we well know, but it's the memory of it that we use to sabotage future endeavors. Why? As I mentioned before, we do this because, ironically, it feels good. Allowing ourselves to feel badly gives us an excuse to feel good, and thus we search for its realization externally, we grant it, and then we feel good. We think that we must only feel badly to be able to feel good…that's the tragedy of the subconscious mind and the rueful game it plays. Thus, we must learn how to reconcile it. How? It starts via this dialogue, this exact conversation. Why? It is bringing the subconscious mind into consciousness via fruitful dialogue. That is the first step: to be aware of its games and to call it by its right name. After this step, the only thing you must fuel is your intention. Do you remember that we have talked about this? About the reality and the power of projecting the honest intention? After you have consciously analyzed what your subconscious mind might be using to sabotage your will (past thoughts, emotions, doubt, guilt, etc.), then you can separate them from the vision you are projecting.

Afterwards, with honest intention, you can ask your subconscious mind to unite with your conscious projection so that what you are willing can be seen completed. As a parallel motive, you ask from your innermost you that if this is right and harmonious in your life plan that it indeed be granted. With this exercise, you have aligned yourself internally (subconscious with conscious) and then taken that alignment and linked it to the divine by asking for the divine hand to paint reality in the way that it will match you and your life perfectly. I hope this helps, my dear brother! Align yourself and start to project, sit back, trust in the divinity, and see how it unfolds!

I love you with all my heart, and today, let me walk with you.

22 Oct
2010

10/22/10

My dearest brother Momo,

I wanted to share with you a beautiful message that I received via email today. I think it encompasses many of the points we have talked about in a beautiful, all-thrilling scene: love. This is my gift to you and your gift to yourself.

Dearest ones, feel it all, deeply. Feel the endless freedom, the bright and shining vision. Taste the certainty of limitlessness and rejoice in your true eternal nature. Feel the power of All I Am rise within you and explode forth as your magnificent Twin Flame heart. Feel the deep assurance that I Am with you always, everywhere you focus, no matter what. Feel how nothing can detain you, how the whole of Creation is your playground, your palace, and as the urge to be creative sparks within your heart, feel also how I provide everything you need to create. In every breath you are fed directly from the Light. Now you are held within my Love.

Feelings are the movements of Creation. I urge you to cherish them and use them to lift you into consciousness and into the resonance of what it means to be this endless burning Love, the power of the cosmos claimed and focused. Feeling is the power of the universe. It is that which moves Creation all by itself. Without the waveform of feeling, the expression of this Love could not occur and you could not unfold as the flower of my Heart.

Everywhere you look, beloved one, I Am. Please let Me in, that I might free you from this dream of separation from Me. Every life on Earth that you have lived has been your search for your return into My arms. Every Love that you have sought in this whole world has really been your heart's call to Me. I Am your Home.

Only when you have found Me can you find true Love, for everything in your life is simply the reflection of your relationship with Me. I Am tender in My Love for you, and I Am personal. Yet, I Am the glory of inspiration. I can show your heart its treasures that are cosmic and I can be for you the Love that fills your nights and brings you peace.

Your heart, beloved one, is the only cathedral that you shall ever need. It is the world's greatest treasure, the most sacred object. All you need to bring you this communion that you ever and always have with Me is to live centered in My Love always.

These are quite precious messages. Mediate on their power and own them.

I love you with all my heart, and today, let me walk with you.

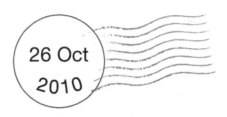

26 Oct
2010

My dearest brother Momo,

I wanted to send a quote your way that came into my life today, and I'll couple it with a few lines from a poem of mine that speaks of the very same principle.

This is the quote: "That which is, already has been; that which is to be, already is; and God seeks out what has gone by" (Ecclesiastes 3:15).

And here is mine:

"What is has been in space that may hold,

A moment born a page, claimed only by a fold."

If you read both of them, but the first one more carefully, you will realize that the beauty of the message lies in a simple truth: it's all in the present. If the present holds the past and what will happen in the future can be conceived in the present, then the present remains the end all and be all, the quintessence of human existence, the absolute only frame of mind we must harbor and fuel. This connects to the other discussions we've had about focusing on the prefrontal cortex... that focusing only takes place in the present and what lingers on, systematically so, is our irrational fixation on the past, which we have already understood as our desire to suffer, because we feel we can only be happy as a result of suffering, through its contrast, and as a post-suffering state. So this is how it all starts to mesh together.

What is fantastic about this quote is that in addition to highlighting how the only attention worth directing is the attention on the present, it also happens that God is who takes care of everything. Therefore, if we focus on the present only, then we can see how the passage says that God will seek out what has gone by. Leave the past to God, focus on the present in order to live the present, and create your future with that energy. Period. We take care of ourselves here and now and thus create the tomorrow, and we let God sift through our past, which we deliver onto him with love and acceptance, for it has brought us right back to today.

If we follow the logical interpretation of this excerpt and the conversations we have had leading up to this point, we will quickly realize that the antidote of suffering is choosing to live in the present. A full and conscious mind, focusing on that which is, will only be able to experiment life as it is happening and will not be able to cling onto emotions, thoughts, analysis—in short, all the very practiced causes of mental anxiety and suffering that focus solely on the past. As a thought experiment, imagine that every thought you have today lives within the space of the "now." Imagine that you could quickly identify, and then immediately erase, all thoughts that somehow point to the past, even if it's a few days or hours ago. What would actually remain? Have we trained ourselves to live so far removed from the present human experience that without rummaging in the past we might actually not have much to think about? How ironic, then, is the sensation of existential freedom?

This thought experiment is not only possible but must be accomplished! We can do this with intention and by simply being conscious of when the past invades the present. If we channel the attitude of self-love and grace, then we will be thankful for the present moment by being witness to the extreme divinity that is fully present in every circumstance and situation, every moment. That attitude, and the recollection of the divine, will obviously leave no real room for suffering but only the appreciation of the human experience as that which is merely happening now. Therefore, that frees us of the past and leaves a beautiful state of mind of love and tranquility: one in which the future we choose to live can begin to be produced in our pre frontal cortex and in recurring ounces of gratitude and self-love. Those are the ingredients and that is the recipe that we must follow to live here today, own tomorrow, and inject love and life into all.

I love you with all my heart, and today, let me walk with you.

27 Oct
2010

My dearest brother Momo,

I just recently started reading this brilliant Sufi master poet named Hafez, and I want to share with you one of his quotes. This quote is the maxim, the quintessence of what it means to be human: to be here today and to truly rejoice in the divine fountain of life. I will, no doubt, be sharing more of his work with you, but let's take a journey into this first one:

"I am a hole in a flute that the Christ's breath moves through—listen to this music."

Aaaah, it just makes me want to keep on breathing! Absolutely grand, right? It absolutely sums up the total human experience—when one allows oneself to connect to the absolute truth. We are here to channel, to play, to facilitate, and to live the music of God's heart. We must be one and the same and then hold similar resources to the divine, if we are able to channel and even propagate the sound of the divine. If this holds, then the recognition of the song, of that divine tune in our external world, must first be preceded by the same internal recognition.

As you are a hole in the flute, I am the hole next to you, and so on and so forth. Humanity claims an independent yet completely communal role in the amplification of God's music. If you drill further, you will realize how the breath of the divine will only be audible, can only be reproduced as musically vibrant, if there is harmony in the holes. The proper position and manipulation of the holes, that is the way in which we choose to live our life and thus the thoughts we choose to give life to, are responsible for turning the divine's breath into music. To hear the divine we must all partake, and one cannot possibly exist without the other, as it is all one and the same, mutually exclusive yet communally dependent on our loving interaction.

To hear the divine we must all partake. What role, then, are we willing to play? Will our hole remain half open or half closed? Will we move closer to other holes in times of need, simply to manifest a more audible and eclectic tune? Will we silence our hole if there is a greater need to listen? And will we know how to let the breath through? The answer to this final question must be the reality we grant ourselves every day of our life. We must ensure that our internal atmosphere is pure and immersed with love, harnessing and fueling only the thoughts of innate divinity which we cherish as gifts, so that we can allow, properly channel, and recognize the channeling of God's divine tune.

I love you with all my heart, and today, let me walk with you.

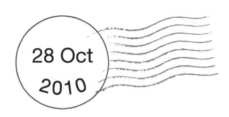

28 Oct
2010

My dearest brother Momo,

I wanted to quote another of Hafez's poems right out of memory, but I am afraid that my memory has failed me today…I will share with you, however, the crux of his poem, which I read yesterday, or at least the essential bits that somehow managed to sink into my soul today. The poem began with a beautiful image: lampposts dangling from the sky, lighting your own way.

It has a beautiful tune to it, because not only are the lampposts suspended from the sky itself, but also their stance is almost celebratory, entirely personal, and always so powerful as it illuminates. As that stanza falls into the next one, the metaphor continues and expands. After you have been illuminated and have recognized that light within, what next? The answer comes in two brief phrases: to just Love, and to just Be Happy. So beautiful.

You have been individually enlightened, and after such, you are left with two simple yet poignant commands: to love and to be happy. The poem then takes a beautiful turn fueled by those two phrases and ends in a powerful claim to life, an exuberant manifestation of reality, and a rapturous call to arms for every single moment to be lived to the fullest: Dance! Dance! Dance! I loved this poem for its exquisite depiction of simple truth…how it all begins with divine illumination: lampposts from the sky, just for you—beckoning you to simply love and be happy—and then culminating in a celebration that once you love and remain happy, you will be able to dance, dance, dance, dance, and dance! It's the free movement of the body, the ecstasy of physical release and freedom that is manifested at the end, all thanks to love and happiness.

I do honestly know for certain that we each have our own lamppost hanging from the sky, but it depends on our wisdom (which is none other than the recognition of the potentiality of this virtue) in order to claim the light as our own. And the beauty that unfolds once we reach the top of this conscious mountain is blessed love and happiness and unity, blessed unity through dance and celebration. My dearest brother, recognize the lamppost that is awaiting your virtuous recollection, and what's more, recognize how you are also a lamppost for many others, shining light where there was none before, aiding others in their own process of internal virtuous recollection, and standing true to the communal strength we all cherish as we dance, dance, dance! I am dancing now, and I can hear your footsteps!

I love you with all my heart, and today, let me walk with you.

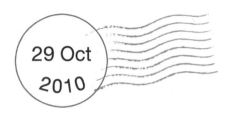

29 Oct
2010

My dearest brother Momo,

I just wanted to clarify something in case there might be the slightest doubt lingering in your mind. Although what we discuss in these emails is essentially directed toward the positive, motivating, and invigorating side of life, it is first and foremost directed to the *real* side of life. I want to underline the reality of this endeavor because that means that there is no good or bad, no better or worse, and most importantly, no expectation arising either from the reflections of these emails or from the thought processes that they may generate.

All that's needed is a perfect loyalty to the present moment, to that which is, to the reality we experience: to the human experience. That means letting everything in, accepting the presence of all thoughts and emotions without rational sieves, and rejoicing in the observation of these mechanisms so as to grow from within. Therefore, remember that the prime interest of all moment's' worth is your complete and conscious appraisal of your human experience. The context in which you are in now will definitely magnify this potential, as everything is new and the day-to-day mechanisms are out of the ordinary.

Therefore, you will incessantly be poked by new insights, emotions, and thoughts that can either govern or simply enlighten your human experience. Choose the latter, and breathe in this life-changing experience with your beautiful smile. I'm not sure if I had commented on this earlier, but one day on the metro in Hong Kong I conjured up this phrase between two friends:

Carlos says first, "Juan, I think the joke is on me," and Juan responds, "Carlos, that is how it seems in certain aspects of life, but remember that we inevitably author the choice of laughter".

How good is a joke without an audience? How good is life without a conscious audience? You are the choice of laughter, and thus you are the laughter itself. This brings us back to the attitude premise, and you can always choose, regardless of what certain aspects of life might or might not show.

But in all these situations, your choice must be focused on acceptance—pure acceptance with gratitude and love—with full trust knowing that it is because it must be, and in that attitude God's light will renew your strength. Let's accept this human experience and observe it as a fellow traveler, as an agent on vacation simmering through the beauty of undaunted human interaction and experience!

I love you with all my heart, and today, let me walk with you.

Part III
November 2010

*What lies behind us and what
lies before us are tiny matters
compared to what lies within us*
Ralph Waldo Emerson

My dearest brother Momo,

Remember the poem I alluded to from the great Sufi master poet Hafiz? Well, I found it,[1] and I will leave you with its infinite rapture and wisdom, so that it may walk with you. Harvest the seed pouch, my dear brother, and immerse your soul in the light of the universal grand order—in His light.

Your Seed Pouch

> *Lanterns*
> *Hang from the night sky*
> *So that your eye might draw*
> *One more image of love*
> *Upon your silk canvas*
> *Before sleep.*
> *Words from Him have reached you*

---

1   Originally discovered at http://www.kerosenequarter.com/post/34210331344/ hafiz.

And tilled a golden field inside
When all your desires are distilled
You will cast just two votes:
To love more
And be happy.
Take these words from the mouth-flute of Hafiz
And mix them into your seed pouch.
And when the moon says,
"It is time to Plant,"
Why not dance,
Dance and sing?[2]

I love you with all my heart, and today, let me walk with you.

---

2 Daniel Ladinsky, *The Gift, Poems by Hafiz* (Penguin, 1999). Reprinted with permission.

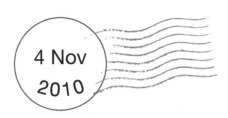

4 Nov
2010

My dearest brother Momo,

I will take this opportunity to share with you two other brilliant poems
by Hafiz that I am sure will hug you deeply and accompany you dearly.
They are gems, and in their verses you will see the own reflection of your
innermost divinity! The first is called "The Violin":

When
The violin
Can forgive the past
It starts singing.
When the violin can stop worrying
About the future
You will become such a drunk laughing nuisance
That God
Will then lean down
And start combing you into
His

Hair.
When the violin can forgive
Every wound caused by
Others
The heart starts
Singing.[3]

With this poem, I know you will once again reunite with your violin and breathe truth to its greatness. Remember you are a wooden hole in the flute of this world, and His music is yours. Being in the present, forgiving yourself, and allowing His light to shine into your world will grant the music you seek.

This next one is called "You're It," and it will remind you to look for God in absolutely everything, with a whimsical smile and the ecstatic dance of a human who sees and listens to the music!

God
Disguised
As a myriad things and
Playing a game
Of tag
Has kissed you and said,
"You're it –"
I mean, you're Really IT!"
Now
It does not matter
What you believe or feel
For something wonderful,
Major-league Wonderful

3   Daniel Ladinsky, *The Gift, Poems by Hafiz* (Penguin, 1999). Reprinted with permission.

Is someday going
To
Happen.[4]

You are something Major-League Wonderful, my brother, and the infinite wonder of this world is found in the first mirror your find yourself facing. Go out and live your Glory!

I love you with all my heart, and today, let me walk with you.

---

4   Daniel Ladinsky, *The Gift: Poems by Hafiz* (Penguin, 1999). Reprinted with permission.

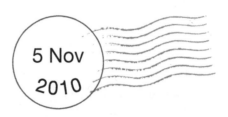

My dearest brother Momo,

We've spoken about attitude, we've spoken about mental projections from the pre-frontal cortex, and we've spoken of love. Now I want to speak more of love, for that is the quintessence and most powerful element that we have to carve the existence we desire. Let me first introduce another recollection, and then I'll tie it back to love and how offering love above all else and always is the most liberating promise of acceptance and potential that we can practice!

What I came to understand is just a very simple exposure of human relationships: when you constantly remind people of what they themselves have not yet been able to accept, you automatically become that mirror they want to do away with as quickly as possible, for it reminds them of their inability or conscious decision not to do and the face that they need to face. Now what happens when you become this mirror, and this can be via conscious choice or simply by holding yourself with so much truth that they recognize what you recognize, is that you inevitably create that distance and space between the individual and their recognition of inability: you. With this comes slight rejection, maybe continued rebellion, etc.

This is the same thing that happens with us by the way, when we shy away from our truth and choose to look the other way. At the end of the day, whether we want to accept it or not, we know, and it's exactly in that moment of recollection that our defense mechanisms kick in and the mental dialogue begins...and everything that keeps us from feeling and connecting to that virtuous moment gets triggered. So what happens when instead we opt for showing a mirror of love, both self-love and external?

If that happens, then what we are actually doing is facing the situation with love—still with reality but with love—and that means acceptance. People will recognize that you recognize their faults or inability, but they will also recognize a parallel acceptance of exactly that—as a normal human characteristic—and so they will stop rejecting, stop fighting, and stop trying to get rid of you as the source of consciousness. What's more, they will magically begin to face these issues, because the space is now acceptance and love, support and companionship, and not a moral judgment of inferiority. That's the ultimate beauty of choosing to reflect love and to be the mirror of reality and consciousness but channeled through the power of acceptance!

I love you with all my heart, and today, let me walk with you.

9 Nov
2010

My dearest brother Momo,

I experienced an epic celebration yesterday: Faithless was here in concert in Mexico City for the first time. Maxi Jazz, the lead singer, is an enlightened soul, and he simply presents himself with the sole intention of offering love and energy: communal transcendence from his position on the stage to your ecstatic dancing position on the floor. It's simply majestic to witness the presence of that kind of beauty and deliverance through music. In one of their songs entitled "We Come One," he asked everyone in the audience to put their index finger up and said, "This used to be the symbol of individuality, but tonight this is our symbol of unity—we come one!" It was simply beautiful, my brother, and I know you would have appreciated his method profoundly.

His message is your message as it is ours, and through this email you can reconnect to that ever-present truth that guides your life! At the end of the concert, he asked us to share all the love that we had created together with as many people as possible. That is exactly the way life should be faced, with the sole purpose of sharing the love you yourself have first decided to generate. If we can't generate it for ourselves first, we will simply keep on falling under the false pretense that love (and everything else we might be searching for) is found on the outside, on that external realm, and not from the inner source of innate divinity we all share. We've inevitably grown so far removed from the essential and basic premises of life that we even forget to cherish the infinite realization of possibility.

We can accomplish anything! It can be absolutely anything, but somehow we forget to channel that acknowledgment to actually rejoice in the reality that we began to design for ourselves in our thoughts. More and more, I believe that life is just a process of somehow reconnecting to that which was ours by birth. It's a process of constant reconnection and reaffirmation, of constant re-, re-, re-, re-everything, because we somehow chose to forget. What if we could decide now that the only re- was the re-decide, and we could decide again, decide now, to re-affirm our re-decision to reconnect constantly and to remember?

That is the only decision we must make: the decision to live freely based on what we have always known to be ours and have the loving courage to share it brightly with everyone! I leave you with this beautiful thought-journey!

I love you with all my heart, and today, let me walk with you.

10 Nov
2010

My dearest brother Momo,

It is a beautiful blessing to be able to write to you. It is not because of the situation, not because of the context, not because of the message, but it is simply because there is a connection between us that can be celebrated through writing. There are so many instances in life, so many corners to negotiate, so many experiences, and yet on and on, we continue to realize that the very important people, those essential souls in our life that mark us, are few and far between. They are jewels in our world, and thus we must cherish them properly.

That is why I salute you today, that is why I joyfully hear my fingers crack at the keyboard, because this letter epitomizes the opportunity of real transcendence in our third dimension by being the realization of a beautiful human connection. This is our gift, my brother, and it's the gift we are able to share with anyone, if they too are willing and able. So, definitely smile and rejoice in the amount of truth that is sent and felt as these words reach you, for that is our reality, and it really makes a difference. I honestly believe more and more that the absolutely best gift you could ever offer is a piece of yourself (as Ralph Waldo Emerson claimed "The greatest gift is a portion of thyself"), an un-sieved, free, careless, and completely loving portion of yourself that will somehow manifest its presence, through acceptance, in someone else's life. That is our most precious gift, and when it's reciprocated, when the magic flows both ways, both souls are elevated continuously beyond recognition.

When that happens, my dear brother, time is never a burden nor distance a hassle, for everything is simply in rapturous communion… through the recollection of something divine shared amongst two loving equals. By harvesting this type of connection in your life, you are opening the doors to your heart and allowing your true self to shine without any limit indeed. You are granting yourself the space to become and then to share the becoming, so that someone else might share it back and further still. At the end of the day, the power of life comes from our power to love: to first love oneself and then to recognize that same love in someone else, and thus to share not its generation but its recognition!

We owe it to ourselves to find the courage to share this particular type of truth. Everything is possible through intention, and the celebration of intentions met is a cause for fireworks!

I love you with all my heart, and today, let me walk with you.

11 Nov
2010

My dearest brother Momo,

I wanted to remind you of something truly wonderful you shared with me back in that glorious summer when our families travelled together through the South of France and Spain. I believe we were trying our luck with the local hotties on that beach in Marbella, wondering what that defining characteristic, that winning strategy might be that would seal the deal, and you simply reminded me of something wonderfully essential…you said, "Just smile man, that's it." There is so much power in that, my brother, and so much worth in its beautiful simplicity.

At that moment, you recognized that the only thing you could possibly do to communicate any ounce of beauty, virtue, truth, intention, etc., was a simple smile. Recognizing that means that you recognize the power inside you: how the simple channeling of it through a smile was actually a smile to yourself. It also means that you have anticipated the glory of sharing…of sharing a smile and that you know that when you share something as precious and simple as that, humans respond well— they respond kindly—for it's a free zone, a non-threatening enterprise, a truly simple human connection. A smile. That's it, brother, just a smile. A smile to open doors, a smile to send love, a smile to understand, a smile to share, and a smile to live. It's truly fascinating how our bodies manifest emotions—how tears come into existence—an insurmountable surge of emotion that needs to escape and cannot possibly be contained any longer and thus transforms itself into a tear that symbolizes our livelihood, the cry of our soul to be heard loud and clear.

A smile, the perfect and very conscious symbol of the face that communicates nothing other than love and joy. I am fascinated by it, because the most important things in life are completely effortless; they simply depend on the intention to allow that moment to happen. That's exactly how seamless and pure a smile is…it lasts maybe a few seconds, but the memory of one can last forever…and what it makes you feel can reach the deepest depth of your humanity. A few seconds, a curvature in the lips, a beam in the eyes: that's the recipe of essential beauty. Wow! And here we go trying to buy the biggest diamond and the grandest house… trying to impress through deeds and purchases, when all we had to do was true, unique, pure, and all-delivering…smile. A piece of ourselves is the most precious gift we can offer. It begins with our decision to allow ourselves to recognize that there is something to give. I smile at you, my brother. I smile brightly.

I love you with all my heart, and today, let me walk with you.

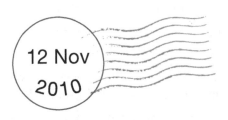

My dearest brother Momo,

Beautiful Friday. There are so many things that we allow ourselves to fall back in love with only because it's Friday. Well at least that's what happens when your Monday through Thursday is drenched in bleaker overtones…but in essence we should celebrate each and every day as a glorious Friday: giving ourselves the right to expand our minds, to open up our hearts, to celebrate, to connect, to share, and to give a bigger, better, more luminous part of ourselves!

I wanted to let you know that I've been practicing the powerful art of the smile all day today…there are times when it's not as easy or times when it doesn't come quite as naturally…but when I feel that, I try to remember the better things, try to fix my mind on the virtuous things, on the blessed memories of good things, and thus I start smiling at myself. First and foremost, I direct my smile internally to my own space of recognition and acceptance, and once I touch that smile, then I start to carve the ones I am ready to share. I've started a new experiment that I will definitely comment further on as the week progresses, because I have yet to deliver myself fully into this complicated endeavor in order to then be able to share the pearls of insight that I gather from its journey. But for now I will introduce the main concept: learning how to invest and give the right percentage of yourself based on each context. This is a very important process for me, because I am so passionate and intense. I like to lose myself, deliver myself, give of myself entirely to the situation and to people, and sometimes the lack of reciprocity really hurts. Therefore, there has to be a way to give of yourself but not all of yourself.

There must be a way to give the parts that you know will be well received based on the giving and accepting potential of the other party. The trick here is not to hold back in anger, regret, or guilt, but to offer the percentage of yourself from a source of love and acceptance with equal acknowledgment of what exactly it is that you can give to that particular context. I think that this is a wise endeavor, because then the joke is no longer on you. Because the person that fails to reciprocate is not doing it personally, it is simply a symptom of their personality, insecurity, fear, etc., and you cannot expect that person to change. You must author your own version of reciprocity, beginning with the realization that people are different when it comes to their willingness and ability to offer a part of themselves! This is good for now. I will keep it coming.

I love you with all my heart, and today, let me walk with you.

My dearest brother Momo,

I do apologize for not having written to you in what appears to be five or six days, but unfortunately I fell ill last Monday, spent half the night in the hospital, and have been recovering since then. Today is the first day back into go-mode, but the world is still spinning slightly. That being said, there is something of far greater worth that I must communicate and that is my deepest and most sincere gratitude, for I know that there is a letter from your hand awaiting me at our grandmother's home.

Due to my illness, I have not yet been able to approach the castle and get my letter, but know full well that not a moment passes without me thinking about it! I need to know from you, and thus my next email to you will hopefully be the email in which I talk about my reaction to your most anticipated letter! Until then, let me just say that it is beautiful to know that that present awaits me, and thus I will delay the pleasure of reading it with a smile on my face, and I thank you once again, truly, for that kind gesture.

There are many things happening in my life right now, and I think I have yet to share with you some of the highlights. The most important is that I am currently finalizing my applications for graduate school. That's it, buddy: graduated almost two years ago, went to Rwanda for about a year for a life-altering experience, came back to Mexico, and now am ready to get back on the academic horse to continue bridging my gaps, so that I can become the high-impact change agent that I dream of. I am applying to the best universities and the best programs out there, and I feel confident that most will have me, and thus I look forward to the dilemma that awaits: having to choose between towering institutions of thought and transcendence, and I hope also, in parallel, for the wisdom to choose wisely! I am going to study Public Administration or Affairs or Policy and International Development or some type of variation therein.

My goal is to change the world, and I know that this will happen. I just need to re-immerse myself into an enabling environment that will push me to excel and instill in me that irrepressible thirst to go out there and become the change that you care for! I love to dream: to dream with the proper stroke of reality, supported by the discipline needed to accomplish that dream, step-by-step, minute-by-minute, and task-by-task. I'll keep you posted!

I love you with all my heart, and today, let me walk with you.

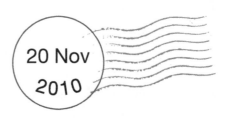

My dearest brother Momo,

I have not yet been able to recuperate your letter, and unfortunately, your sister came and left without me seeing her, but I promise that the next letter I write will contain my reception and reflection of yours. I kind of like putting it off…it's that implacable, pleasure-delaying principle which I adore…such a precious gift awaits, and I will sink into it completely, fully, and wholeheartedly. I just recently read an email, a PowerPoint of sorts, that sort of briefly encapsulated the entire spectrum of eastern philosophy…the main point that it made was that any suffering comes from the prior formulation of an expectation, and when people, events, situations, or circumstances obviously fail to meet the expectation, we take it personally, and thus we suffer, because we feel that the person, event, situation, or circumstance actually committed the act intentionally.

I support that premise, and I am sure you have discussed its reality in your internal world as well. What I also want to comment on is that it is not always an expectation that governs the "suffering" quota, and what the person did should not always be excused or not seen for what it is (regardless of the person's conscious intention to do so) simply because we just happened to have a contradicting and fairly impossible expectation in our minds. If we feel whatever we feel as a product of something that someone has done, said, shown, etc., it is probable that we might suffer due to a prior expectation, even if as simple as "I didn't expect that person to do x or y," but that doesn't excuse the x or y.

I am trying to call back our attention to the principle of reality, to the governing essence of that which is, so that we don't evade simply because we expected…I do agree that nothing should be taken personally, as much as possible, because we all act sometimes completely in disarray with our beliefs or what we have said or done before, but we cannot fail to see the act for what it is, call it what it actually is, and then simply decide what we will do about it in that context. I think this distinction is necessary, because it not only will save us from taking things personally but also from failing to acknowledge and accommodate the reality of the situation. Accommodating the reality will then allow us to retaliate with a fruitful response: one built on reality and the recognition of that reality. That's it!

I love you with all my heart, and today, let me walk with you.

Part IV
Momo's Letter

*Not until we are lost do we
begin to understand ourselves*
Henry David Thoreau

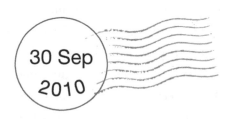

30 Sep
2010

HMP Liverpool, UK
Querido Ale hermano,

It would be nothing short of unacceptable for me to start this letter off
with anything other than my genuine gratitude for every single email
that I have received from you. In these I have found great compassion,
companionship, love, and support all embedded in the wise insights
you so generously share. Now I want you to know that I feel the love,
the support, and most of all, the priceless encouragements you send
my way.

Indeed bro, this situation I find myself in is rather heavy on the
mind. But like any other muscle in the human body, the counter-pressure
we exercise towards the weight we face is what will eventually develop
strength, substance, and perseverance. When I first came in, I was in a
state of mind similar to a bad day in depression. As they say, the mind
is a chariot driven by wild horses. But shortly enough, between the time
I was transferred from the court prison to my holding prison, through
prayer and thanksgiving, the horses were tamed, and my journey began.

It's difficult to explain the peace that I have found in the certainty that God has been and will be with me and within me, all the way of this. At night, my mind is quiet and my body still. During the day I feel alert, but in a peaceful way, as if I have been given an opportunity to access a certain perspective of life, society, and the human mind, all while sitting on the sideline. However, the smile only works to a certain extent, for during certain times I play an active part in the scenario.

There is a deep truth in what you mention about our ability to author any given perspective of a situation. It's funny that you elaborate so much on the matter; one of the first truths made evident to me in this place is the human mind's capability of authentically "convincing" itself of a perspective in a given situation. With a vast array of circumstances bordering a situation, it is the choice of focusing on some circumstances rather than others that give way to such a variety of perspectives, alternates to a central situation. Now, the intrinsic truth behind this realization is found in the knowledge that God is not bound by circumstance. Hence, by recognizing the seed of eternity, what you refer to as the "inner divinity" that God has planted within us, we tap into the essence of true human experience beyond circumstance. As these boundaries fade, we gain a more substantial insight of the present, not bound to the past or shaped by our attempt to mold the future.

I particularly love the comparison you make between suffering and pain with regards to a bump on the head. Very true, my brother. In a similar way, enslaving emotions such as hate, bitterness, and contempt are always so subtly misconstrued. We tend to believe that by holding someone in contempt, we are actively balancing out the pain they caused us. On the contrary, contempt will only cause further pain to the one who holds it, further "suffering" by bounding him to something that is no longer. I, for one, am grateful for the time I spent on bail prior to my incarceration. For it is during that time that God guided me, regardless of the outcome of the court case, to forgive and by doing so, to release myself from any stronghold of the past. So, bitterness and contempt gave way to peace, understanding, acceptance, and the potential to grow.

There's something that struck me when reading the words of the Sufi poet Rumi. This concept of a root is so familiar yet so ignored by so many of us. Over the years, through one experience after another, we have buried this youthful root with an array of rational human constructs that eventually leave this root, this Divine light, buried beneath a thick surface: a surface we then ironically call "ourselves." Primo, as you say, God has given me the priceless opportunity to go back to this root, to dig up all the soil left behind by a lifetime of investing in the mind's ego, to reunite with the soul's light.

Rumi mentions or suggests that we find the antidote in the venom. To this, I allow myself the vernacular: WORD, SON! That is exactly what I seek now. And as you say, it all comes down to choice. Daily, I wake up and choose to see the beauty in the mess. In the words of Charles Baudelaire: "you gave me your mud and I turned it into gold." Through acceptance, I can see the fertilizing nature of the dirt, and I chose to sow nothing but seeds of positive growth.

Finally, I'd like to say a word on Nietzsche's theory of Eternal Recurrence. Having spared me the undoubtedly intricate ins-and-outs of the theoretical construct, you've left me with a beautiful concept full of truth and perspective. Living each day under this impression of its eternal recurrence brings forth a presence within us, aligning our mind, body, and soul with the everlasting present. That is beautiful, Chocho. It does lay a certain amount of unnecessary weight on the decisions we take daily, but that leads to the choice you mention: you choose to see this as either binding or liberating; it's all down to you. It also brought my attention to the time we waste entertaining negative thoughts and how, if we saw that process under the light of Nietzsche's theory, we wouldn't be so careless as to tread on negative thoughts.

This reminds me of something my gymnastics coach used to tell me when training me on dismounting the bar or the vault, or doing a summersault. He would always remind me to fix my eyes on the exact spot of the landing, for wherever my eyes were set, that is where I would end up. So I bring this into life; if we keep our mental eye focused on "trippin' the dark side," that will eventually be our destination. On the other hand, if we fix our gaze on beauty, potential and positivity, we invite ourselves to greater destinations.

Anyways, Primaso, I hope you've been enjoying all your music gigs. I am very jealous, my friend, but we'll be jamming soon. Also, I'm glad to hear you're attempting to balance out the extremes of your weekend and weekdays. Living in the extremes creates unnecessary pressure between the two poles. Tread the grey arena brother. I love you dearly, I miss you greatly, and I look forward to your next email. You are hugely appreciated, bro. And today, let me appreciate your company as we walk on.

Momo

Part V
The Last Letters

For a man to conquer himself is
the first and noblest of all victories
Plato

22 Nov
2010

My dearest brother Momo,

Thank you so very much for your letter! I was finally able to pick it up, and I saved it for a moment of pure relaxation and joy yesterday evening. You have no idea how beautiful it felt to finally feel you closer, to finally hear from you and understand your perspective, and to finally, finally, have the connection sealed and felt.

I want to share with you my initial impressions of both your letter and your person in general, for without proper contrast and perspective on where you are, I can anticipate how it might be easy to lose sight of one's self. Let me begin by expressing my sincere, overarching joy, for I know that you are owning this experience to the fullest extent, that you are a responsible author in search of that which is, and that you have found a way to focus your attention on the divine: on the presence of God in everything and on the truly essential. I have always told you that you are a blessed warrior poet. In your letter, the prose of your courage, of your heart, of your love, and above all of your integrity came through in blinding colors. I am awestruck and greatly amazed by your composure, both internal and external, and by the serenity with which your wisdom and messages came through.

To be able to write as you did, you must live as you do, for it's all a reflection of an inner state of something. Therefore, I rest assured knowing that you have found the essential in your context, and you have used it to deliberately author a reality that is well worth living, enjoying, and even rejoicing in. You have allowed yourself to do what very few do: transcend your most immediate surrounding in search, and in prior recognition, of the essential. There is so much courage in that existential drive — the courage of a true warrior poet —and it is precisely that strength of character and that moral fortitude that will guide your path from this day forward, endlessly, profoundly, and always, always in dear company. Many more would have opted for the path of the victim, the powerless victim who forgets that everything is as it should be and thus focuses his attention on blaming the external circumstance instead of recognizing first responsibility and then virtue within.

This is all easier said than done, my brother, and thus I ask you not to take these words lightly, for their source is one of ecstasy, profound respect, and above all, celebration! Today, you must give yourself a hug; you must recognize this valiant worth and celebrate your strength, your resilience, your emotional and mental fortitude, and your faith. Hug yourself from the inside out and recognize that virtue, that strength, which I saw in every punctuation of your letter. Never was a dull thought pronounced, and never a negative emotion displayed. That means that your attention is not suffocated or focused on those aspects of your life, and that, my dear brother, is a cause of celebration.

You are linked to the essential without disregarding the reality, yet still in search for the truth—that truth that springs from an internal order and source of divine wisdom, which you have chosen to see represented, fully and powerfully, in your external circumstance. This is the work of an existential magician, my dear brother, of a wise and humble soul who has duly internalized that suffering has no legitimacy in your life unless you wrongly assume so and that your path remains crowned by the capacity to immerse your soul in endless transcendence and thus in true connection with the innately divine. I am celebrating your story, and I thank you for having me as a spectator and for inviting me to continue walking with you. Our strides have been parallel for a long time, and now they are synchronized by love and virtue. Take them as you continue authoring this valiant poem of overcoming, resilience, and truth. Today can be your everyday, simply turn your view to the inside and rejoice in your beautiful recognition!

I love you with all my heart, and today, let me walk with you.

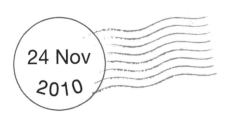

24 Nov
2010

My dearest brother Momo,

I'm still surfing the beautiful emotions that your letter gave me and how good it felt to finally hear from you and to know that my letters were reaching you and reaching you well. I wanted to comment on the brilliance of letting go. The thought is simply a reminder of our inevitable impermanence in this world (in the physical arena), which draws attention much closer to the essential realm, to the divinity, and to the impermanent. Talking about this brings a vision to mind that illuminates the principle beautifully in practice: the Buddhist tradition of making mandalas. I'm not sure if you're familiar with the topic or if you've seen it in movies or shows, but basically a mandala is an offering, through conscious reflection, of our impermanence. A mandala is a beautiful form of art consisting of painted dust arranged in symbolic patterns that represent many different things....

The important point here is that the mandala takes a very long time to make; it is a very detailed and painstaking process, arranging all the small dust particles in a perfect format. And the entire point of the mandala is to be able to see it vanish and thus disappear completely in a matter of seconds by a gust of wind or simple human mistake. Therefore, Buddhist monks are reminded, through the arduous contrast of building the mandala and simply watching how a gust of wind destroys it, of the impermanence of it all in this world and of not placing oneself too close to material possessions, for they are never ours, and they simply represent an impermanent state as well. Now that the theoretical premise is gone, I can introduce what I would like to share regarding the premise of letting go. When I say this, I am not referring to material possessions but to a state of mind and to the internal realization of a divine order and a why and because in all aspects of ourselves. To be able to let go means one is able to trust selflessly in the outcome, but most importantly, it means that one is willing and able to observe how there is no preconceived outcome and thus place oneself in the center of an ever-changing, elusive, and constantly evolving existence which still continues being guided by a divine path.

Letting go means also letting go of all sense of ownership, actual possession, and thus expectation. It means, "letting go and letting God," so that we can once again assume our faithful position as spectators and see the virtue of a life well lived without our constant, incessant intervention. Letting go is a wonderful attitude, for it frees us of ourselves and allows us to simply focus on the two aspects of life so difficult to us humans: to live and to be human. Remember that I had mentioned that we are human beings not human doings? If we harbor a mentality of letting go, then we have already recognized our inalterable internal worth, for by opening up to the whims of the universe, we know that regardless of what might change on the external front, our divine integrity remains on the internal front. Therefore, my dear brother, touch your heart and with gratitude deliver, open up, and let go to let God. Watch the splendid dance of life take place, as we kindly smile in the forefront!

I love you with all my heart, and today, let me walk with you.

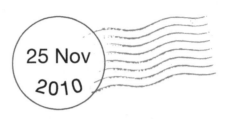

My dearest brother Momo,

I wanted to share something that just came to mind because I was reading something regarding "Entrepreneurial Thought and Action" from my university. I remember I was once asked to define what entrepreneurial thought and action meant to me. I took it a step further and wrote my entire thesis regarding this same dilemma, and I would like to share with you some of the main points, simply because the entrepreneurial path, as you will see, applies to everything: to musicians and to absolutely all walks of life, not just starting a business. In my thesis, I used philosophers and a thorough philosophical exploration to prove that there was an essential cognitive dissonance between risk and reward as means for fueling entrepreneurial thought and action.

Basically, I wanted to show that real, hard-core entrepreneurs didn't assume risks because they found the reward solely in the actual starting of the business or endeavor, but instead found more reward in the process of attaining just that. The real reward was found in the journey, regardless of the final outcome. Therefore, I stated that entrepreneurship is the process of existential creative destruction, whereby an entrepreneur decides to break with an established existential order (a steady job, etc.) to create new existential meaning. That is exactly why the process of starting something, be it a painting, a movie, or a business, so long as it is entrepreneurial, proves so personally significant, promising, and essentially life changing—because you are definitely changing your life!

Consequently, deciding to become an entrepreneur or to ride the entrepreneurial rollercoaster will yield enormous existential benefit, for everything is new. You are assuming new roles, you are outside your comfort zone, you are developing skills and characteristics that you hadn't before, and, what's most important, you are stimulated intellectually and existentially, and thus you are alive! As a result, you can see how the process of starting, of initiating, of beginning is the process of creating, starting, initiating, and beginning new existential meaning. Entrepreneurs understand the fundamental notion that change is life's constant and that only by remaining flexible, intuitive, and intrigued by change will one be able to maneuver it successfully. I'd even go far enough to say that entrepreneurs create change; they anticipate movement and initiate chaos simply to keep the wheels churning and to constantly fuel the existential fire. I share this with you, because today you are an existential entrepreneur, and you are painting your new shades of meaning. Immerse your soul into the process!

I love you with all my heart, and today, let me walk with you.

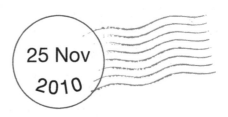

My dearest brother Momo,

Today is a beautiful day. It is Thanksgiving, and it is a wonderful privilege, as I already said in a prior email, to be able to give thanks for you. When we have nobody to thank, it means that we have failed to open our eyes or engage in any type of two-way connection, interaction, and thus human development. Today is that day of the year when we are compelled to be thankful, in which we can fuel an attitude of gratitude, because it's okay and everybody is doing it. Today should actually be a day in which we remain equally thankful, just like any other day, yet we also acknowledge the power of communal gratitude and are thus compelled not to just remain grateful but to share that gratitude with those closest.

That I think is the true worth of this day: the ability to share communally and to rejoice in the very transcendental feeling and life-attitude of gratitude. And that my dear brother, I think, is the true worth of life. So let's not celebrate Thanksgiving, but our unyielding ability to always embody an attitude of gratitude and intrinsic worth and to have the intention of sharing just that! I want to thank you for being in my life, for being an outstanding source of connection, love, understanding, companionship, and friendship. Even in the absence of physical proximity or continuous communication, I learn from you. I learn from you, because you represent so much, because your life is a symbol, and because through my reflections of your life, you share with me your unspoken messages.

Therefore there is nothing that we need: only the intention of connecting, and that will surpass all obstacles. I invite you thus to fuel the attitude of gratitude today, to recognize the existential hiatus that you have been granted to reconnect with the divinity—with the intrinsic power—and to do this for yourself and by yourself, all the while enabled by tremendous sources of companionship and love. Before anything, however, before you can begin to seek sources for which to remain grateful in the external arena, turn your eyes inward and recognize all that you must be grateful for in your internal space. Be thankful for all that you have accomplished, for the life you have allowed yourself to live, for your courage, for the blessings you have given yourself and granted to others, for your serenity, for your wisdom, for your consciousness, and for your maturity. Thank yourself for granting your soul this experience it needed to continue evolving, so that you could once again renew your life force and share it brightly. Thank yourself, as I thank you.

I love you with all my heart, and today, let me walk with you.

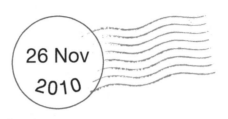

26 Nov
2010

My dearest brother Momo,

I wanted to briefly comment on one thing I've been thinking about now, and then I'll develop it further next week, as I feel it approach. There is quite an ironic element in life with a subconscious source in the human psyche. Basically, and ironically, what we fear the most (and not exactly as horror movie dread but actual existential fear of experimentation or our recognition of inability) is what we end up projecting in our life. I am still not quite sure why this is, but it follows the same principle as projecting that which you actually do desire. Therein lies the real question: if we are projecting that which we apparently do not desire and fear, but it still happens, then must we not desire it silently? Subconsciously? Unknowingly? The real point here is to simply remain conscious of that which we are harboring unconsciously as the worst fear, or as a very imminent fear, in our life. I have a superficial answer at this point, and it follows the same procedure as before. Because we fear it, we are constantly aware of it, even if it is subconsciously.

Therefore, our attention centers on that situation, and thus our energy is constantly channeled towards its visualization, reflection, internalization, comprehension, etc. As we well know, the mind does not discriminate between "good" or "bad," between that which we fear and that which we desire; it simply responds to a continuous channeling of attention, energy, and vivid projection. Therefore, the mind will find resources to portray our worst fears...and I believe that we desire this subconsciously, so that our soul can experience it, learn from it, and thus let it go as just another twirl in its constant evolution. The beauty of all of this is that it can be stopped, simply through intention. If we can identify and anticipate that which we are probably projecting subconsciously, then we can author a different internal dialogue and thus stop the fearful image from being replicated in reality. Otherwise, we can at least identify its replication in reality and choose to do something about it. I think this is a very valuable tool that we can begin to be aware of, so that we choose wisely where we channel our attention!

I love you with all my heart, and today, let me walk with you.

29 Nov
2010

My dearest brother Momo,

I want to share with you something beautiful: the definition of a true "lifester," of someone that injects himself so far into life that all he can encompass is the vast pleasure of living and being human, of the natural state of existence re-defined, and of the innately divine inhaled in every aspect of our precious reality. This is an excerpt from Charles Baudelaire's "The Painter of Modern Life":

"For the perfect idler, for the passionate observer it becomes an immense source of enjoyment to establish his dwelling in the throng, in the ebb and flow, the bustle, the fleeting and the infinite. To be away from home and yet to feel at home anywhere; to see the world, to be at the very centre of the world, and yet to be unseen of the world, such are some of the minor pleasures of those independent, intense and impartial spirits, who do not lend themselves easily to linguistic definitions. The observer is a prince enjoying his incognito wherever he goes.

The lover of life makes the whole world into his family, just as the lover of the fair sex creates his from all the lovely women he has found, from those that could be found, and those who are impossible to find, just as the picture-lover lives in an enchanted world of dreams painted on canvas. Thus the lover of universal life moves into the crowd as though into an enormous reservoir of electricity. He, the lover of life, may also be compared to a mirror as vast as this crowd: to a kaleidoscope endowed with consciousness, which with every one of its movements presents a pattern of life, in all its multiplicity, and the flowing grace of all the elements that go to compose life. It is an ego athirst for the non-ego, and reflecting it at every moment in energies more vivid than life itself, always inconstant and fleeting."

Let's immerse ourselves in that state of passionate observation. Let's become the kaleidoscope and reflect the energy more vividly than life itself!

I love you with all my heart, and today, let me walk with you.

Printed in the USA
CPSIA information can be obtained
at www.ICGtesting.com
JSHW082352140824
68134JS00020B/2027